CW01372000

Disney AFFIRMATIONS

---- ★ ----

positive mantras
· TO BRING ·
Disney magic
TO EVERY DAY

First published in the UK in 2024 by Studio Press,
an imprint of Bonnier Books UK,
4th Floor, Victoria House, Bloomsbury Square, London WC1B 4DA
Owned by Bonnier Books, Sveavägen 56, Stockholm, Sweden
www.bonnierbooks.co.uk

Copyright © 2024 Disney Enterprises, Inc. All rights reserved. Pixar
properties © Disney/Pixar Hudson Hornet is a trademark of Chrysler LLC.

All rights reserved. No part of this publication may be reproduced or
transmitted in any form or by any means, electronic, or mechanical, including
photocopying, recording, or by any information storage and retrieval system,
without permission in writing from the publisher.

1 3 5 7 9 10 8 6 4 2

ISBN 978-1-83587-023-5

Edited by Frankie Jones
Designed by Alessandro Susin
Production by Giulia Caparrelli

MIX
Paper | Supporting
responsible forestry
FSC® C104723
FSC
www.fsc.org

A CIP catalogue record for this book is available from the British Library
Printed and bound in China

Disney

AFFIRMATIONS

— ★ —

positive mantras
· TO BRING ·
Disney magic
TO EVERY DAY

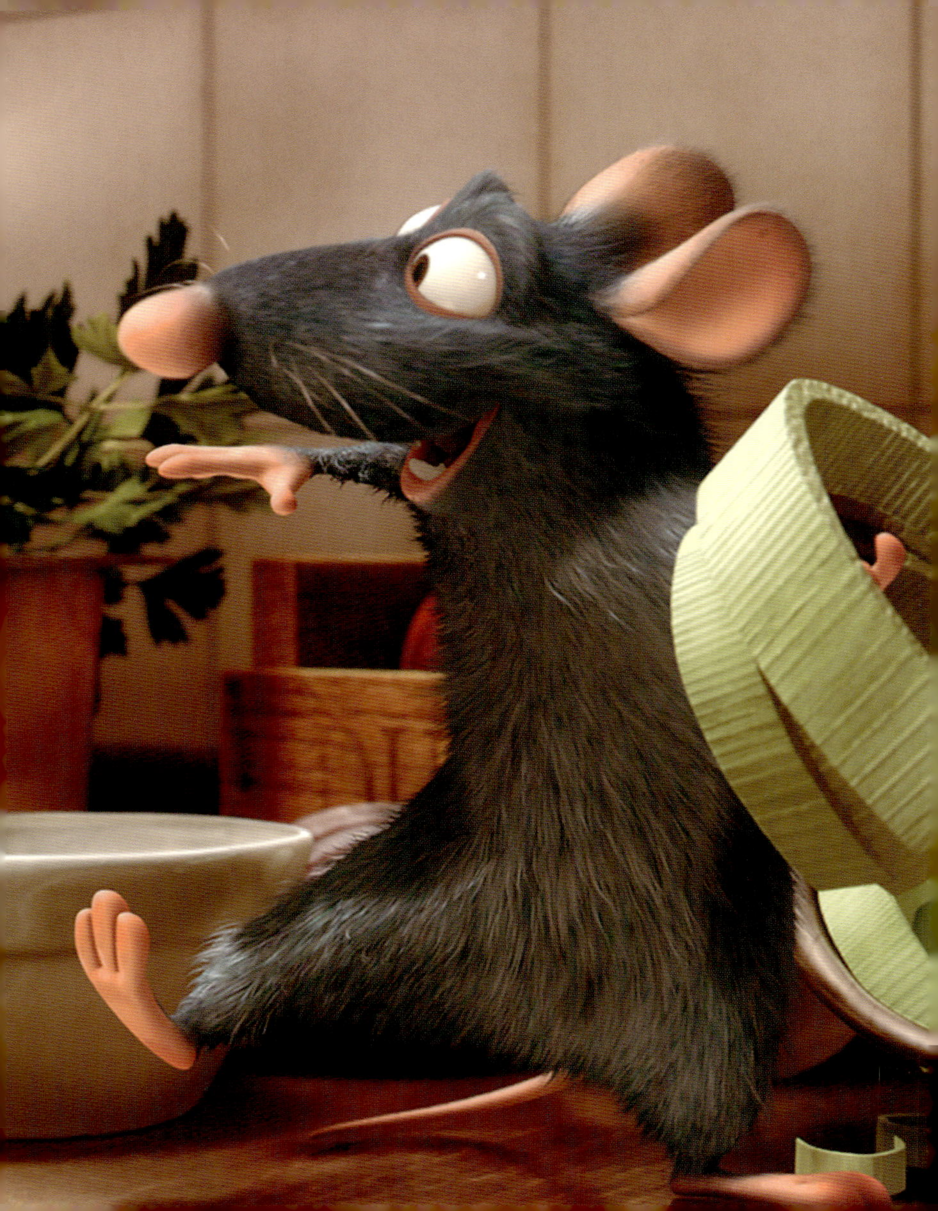

I believe in myself.

★

Discover your "inner why". Find what inspires and excites you, and proudly follow your own unique path.

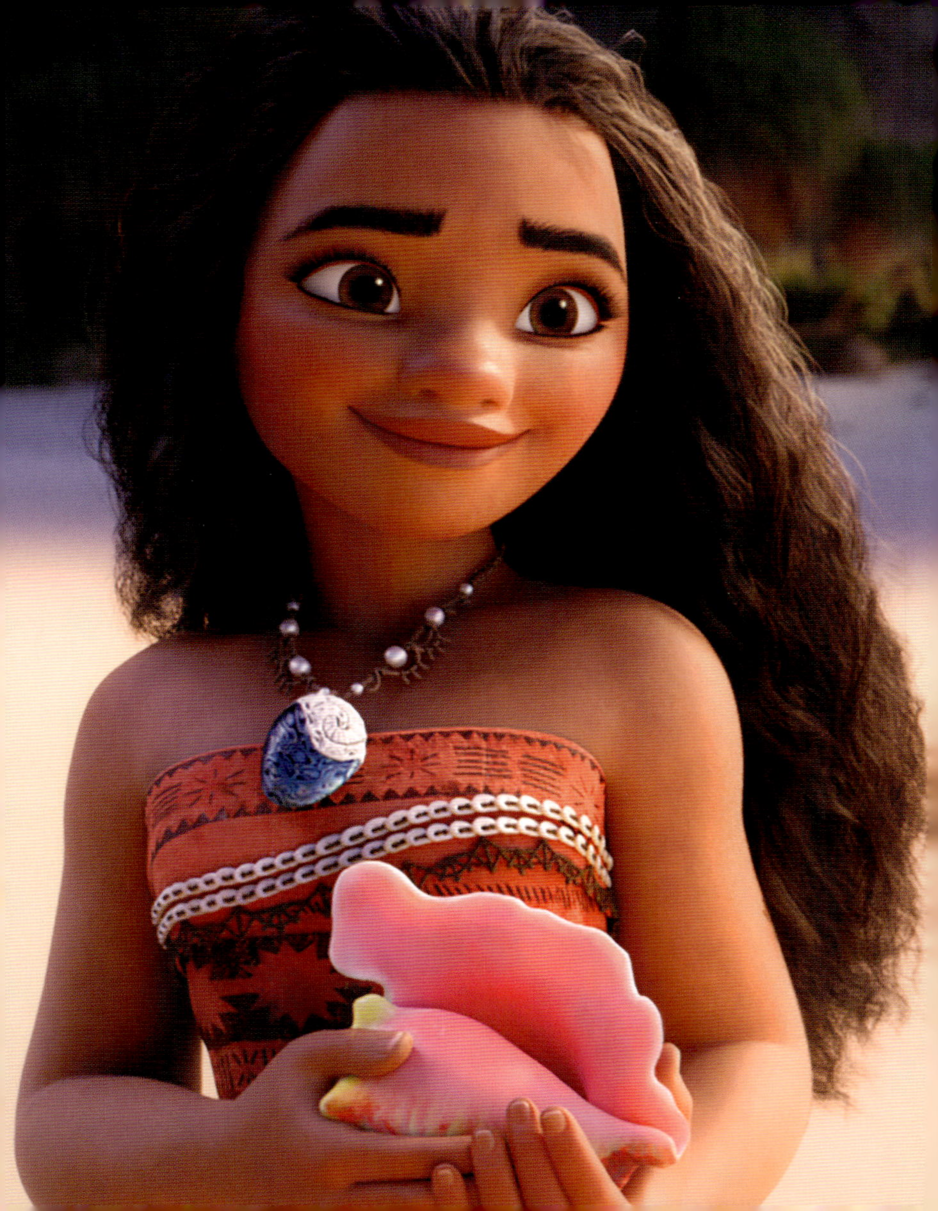

I let go of fear and embrace adventure.

★

The future is like the sea: restless, wonderful, mysterious. Hold on to what you truly believe, and you will overcome every fear and enjoy the greatest adventure of all: your life.

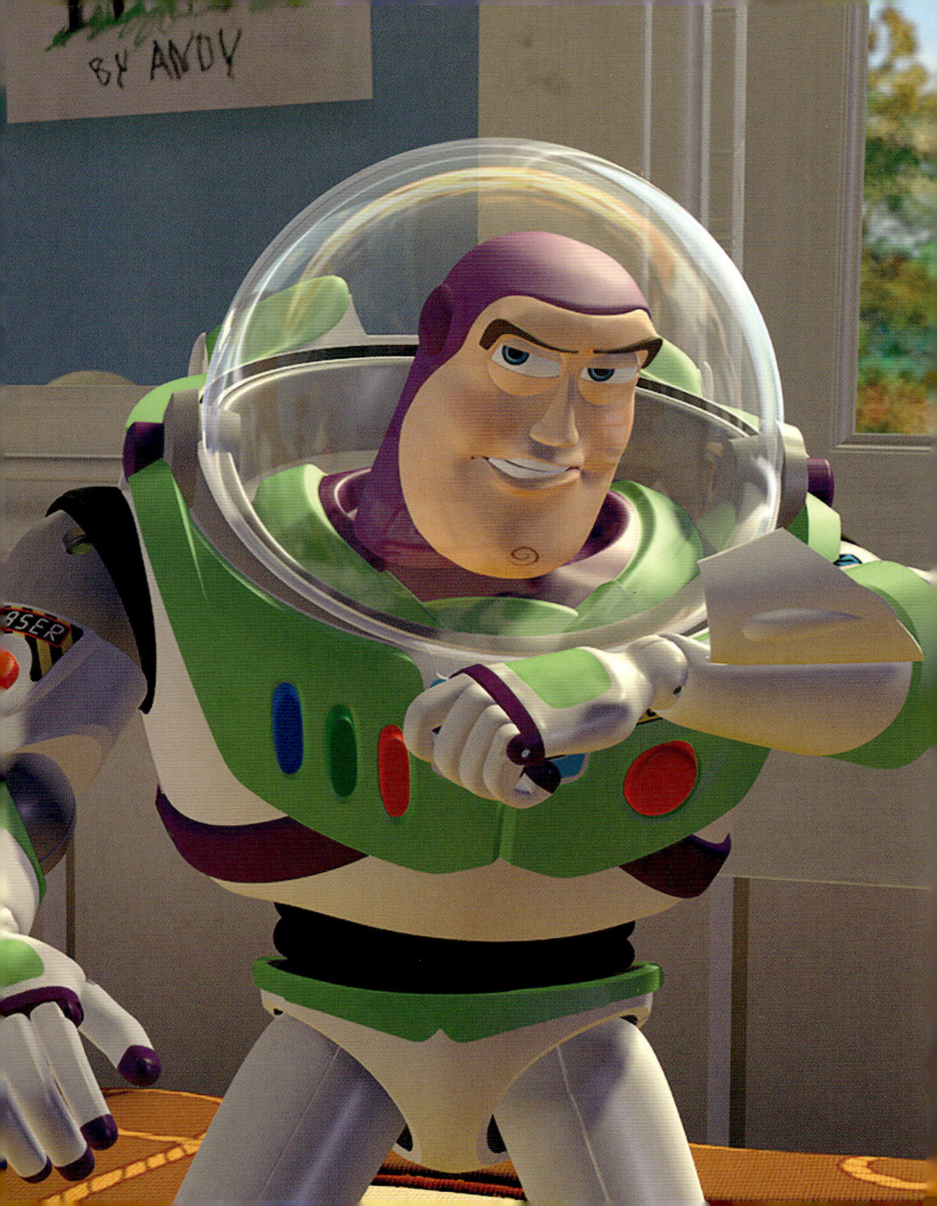
BY ANDY

There is no limit to my potential.

★

Aim high to reach your true potential. To be human is to dream, desire and imagine. Reach out for the impossible, and you will grasp it.

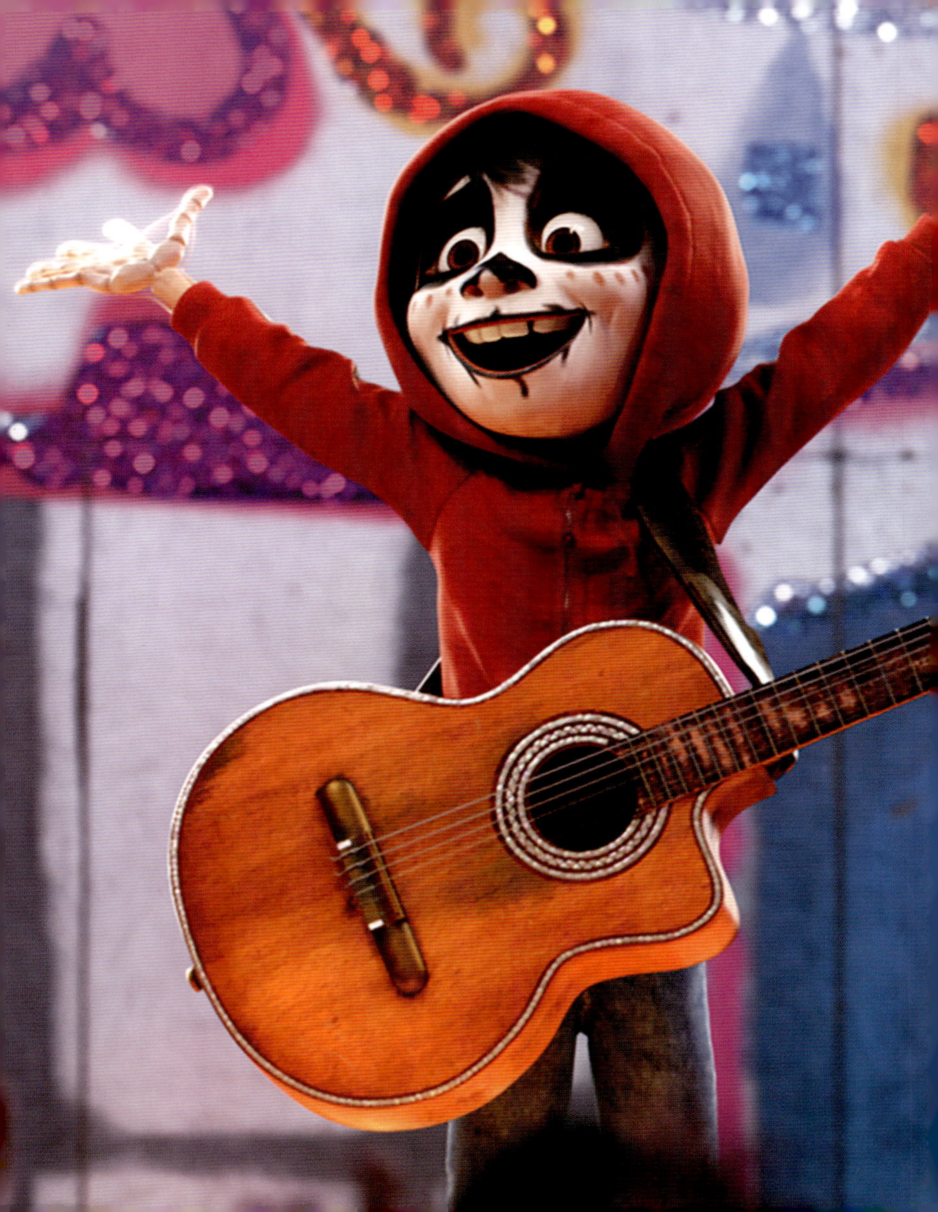

I hold those I love in my heart, and they give me strength.

★

Not every life is filled with extraordinary innovations or heroic deeds to remember. But the care and generosity you share with those around you will never fade. We are immortal in the love of others.

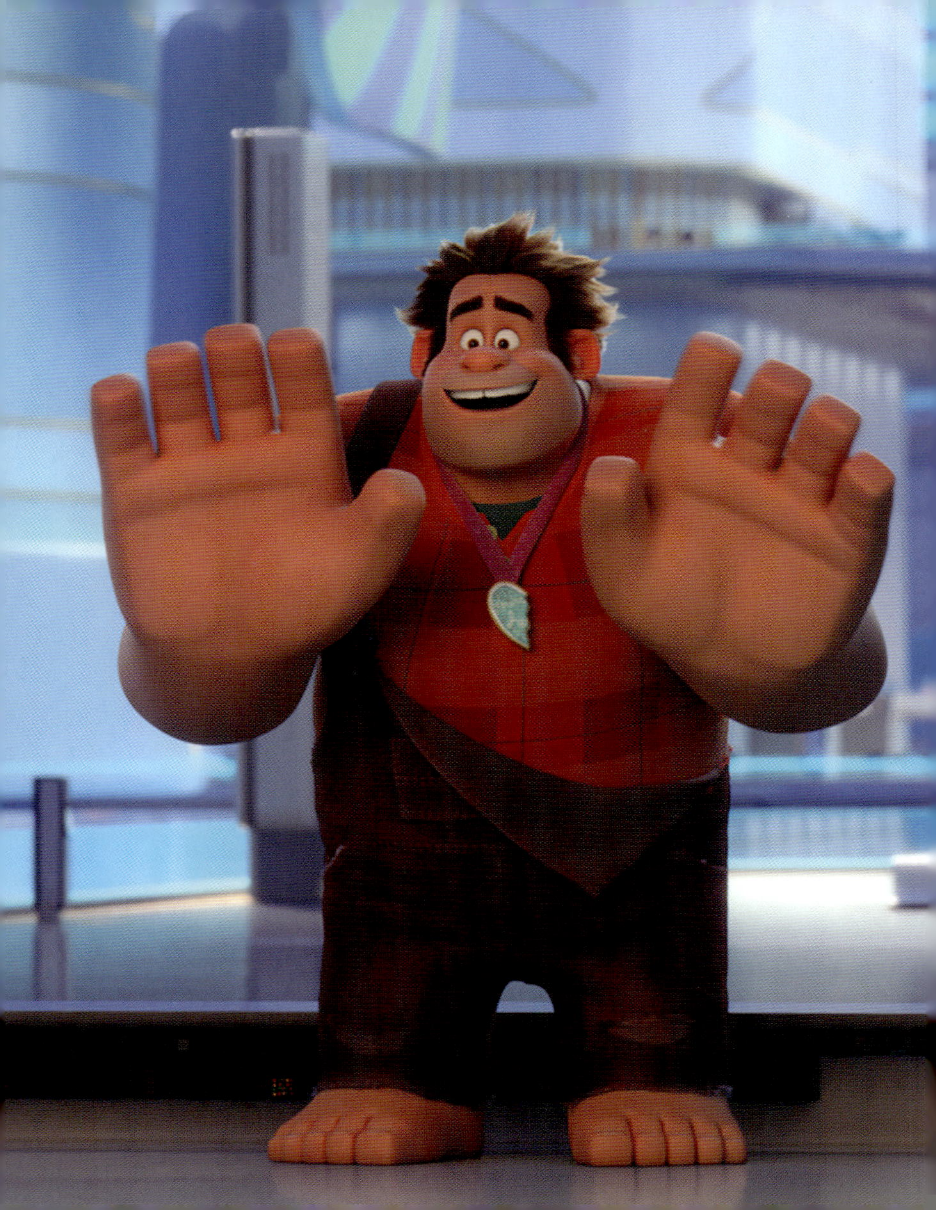

I trust my heart.

★

Our identity is also defined by the looks, words and attentions of those around us. The relationships and experiences we encounter in life contribute to shape who we are and who we will become.

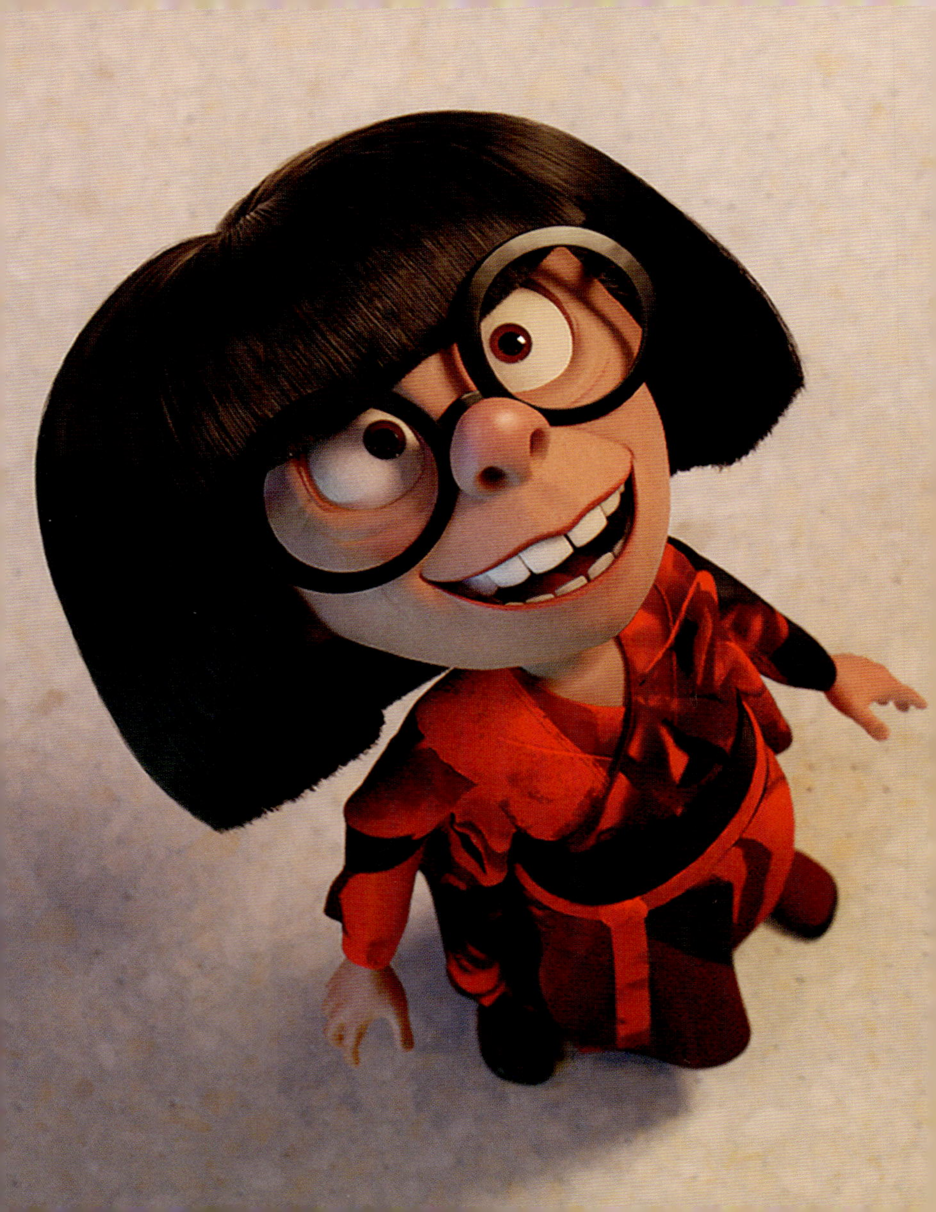

Today's ambition is tomorrow's success.

★

Live in the here and now. Focusing on the present empowers us to make sense of the past and build a future in which we can find ourselves.

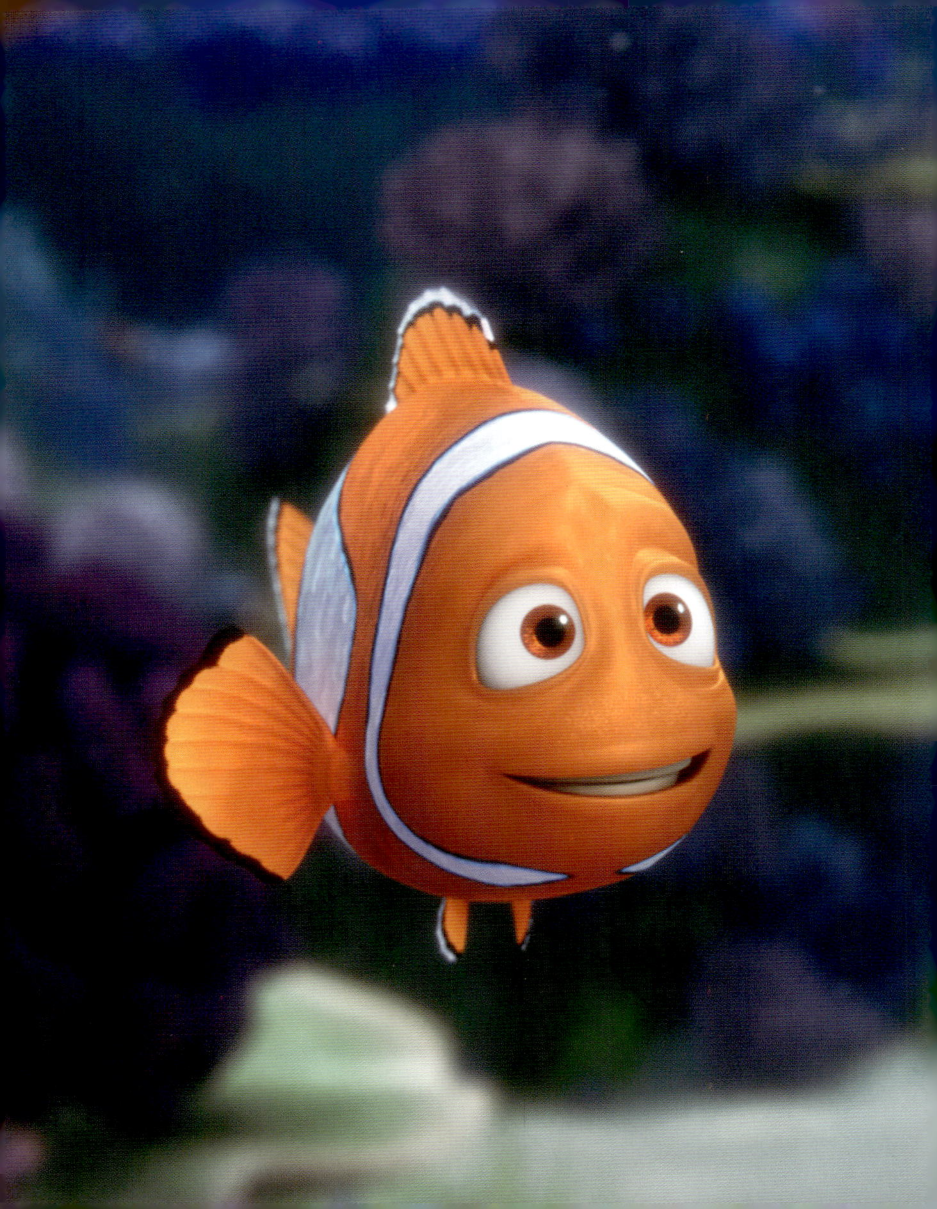

I trust those I am closest to.

★

Be open to the distinct qualities of those around you. While their ideas may not always seem like the obvious answer, looking at things from another angle often leads to the solution.

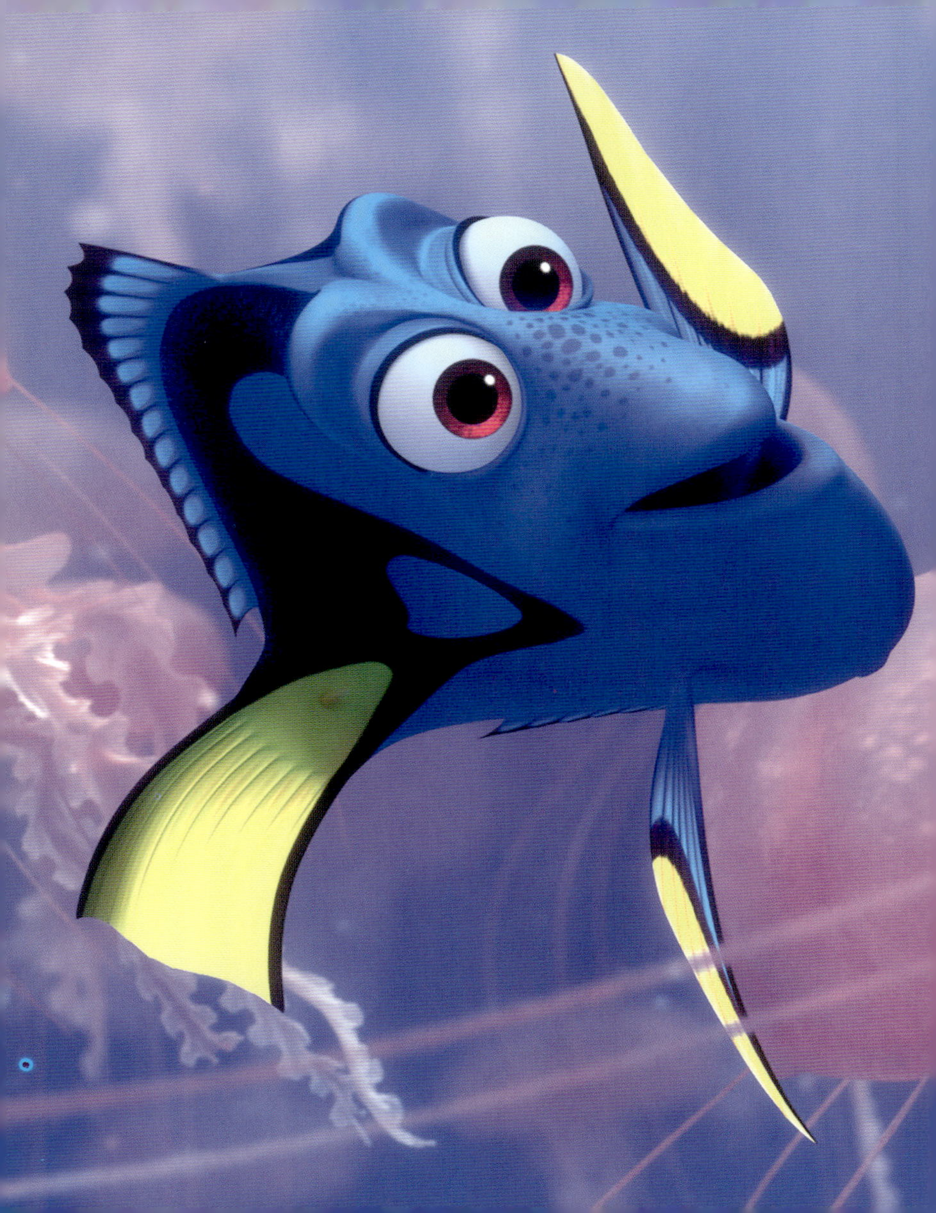

I accept the things that I cannot control.

★

Many things in life are beyond our control. Let go a little and have faith that things will work out. Attempting to constantly direct events can lead to frustration.

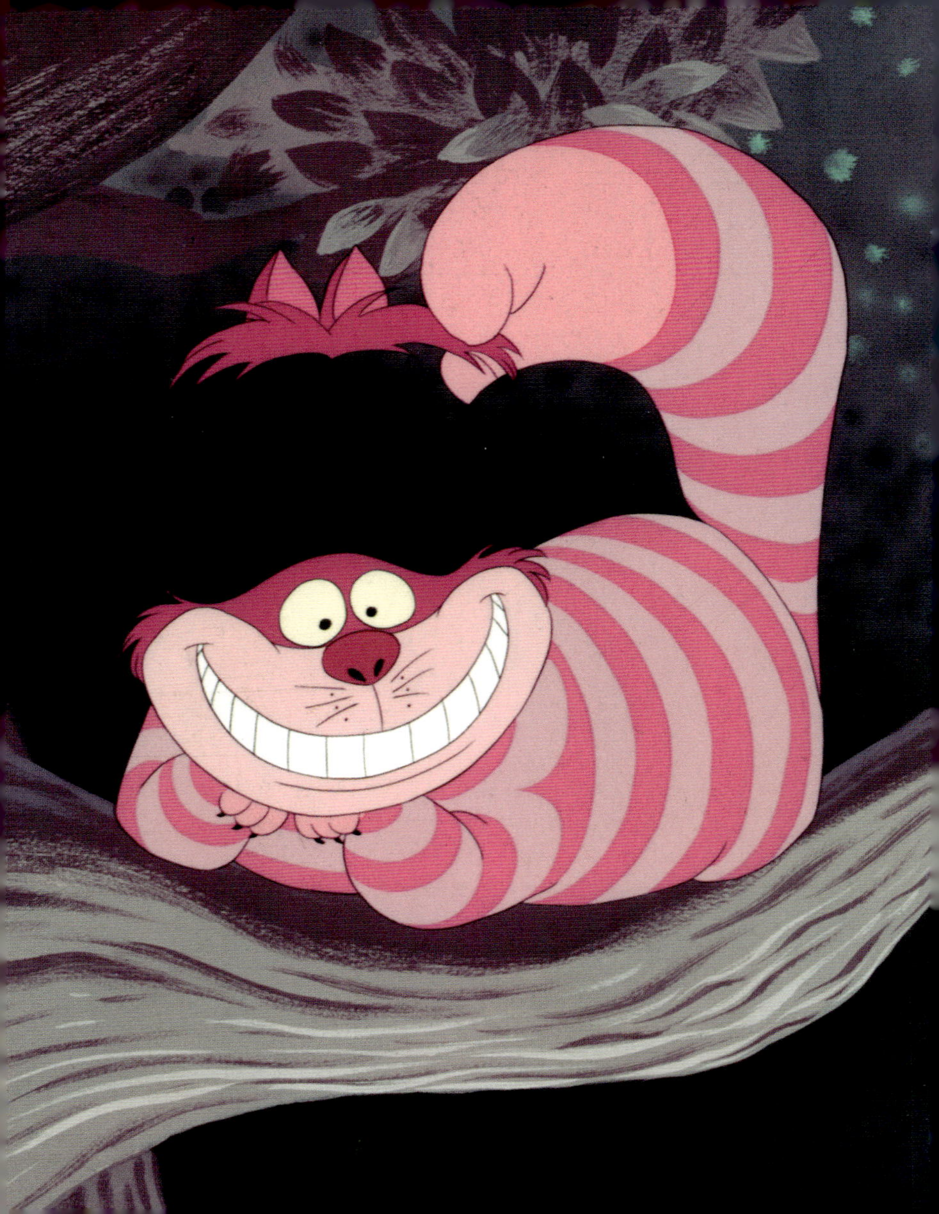

I am open
to different
opportunities.

★

Unconventional people can lead you to experiences you had never imagined. Explore their unusual perspectives, and you will open your eyes to a brand new world.

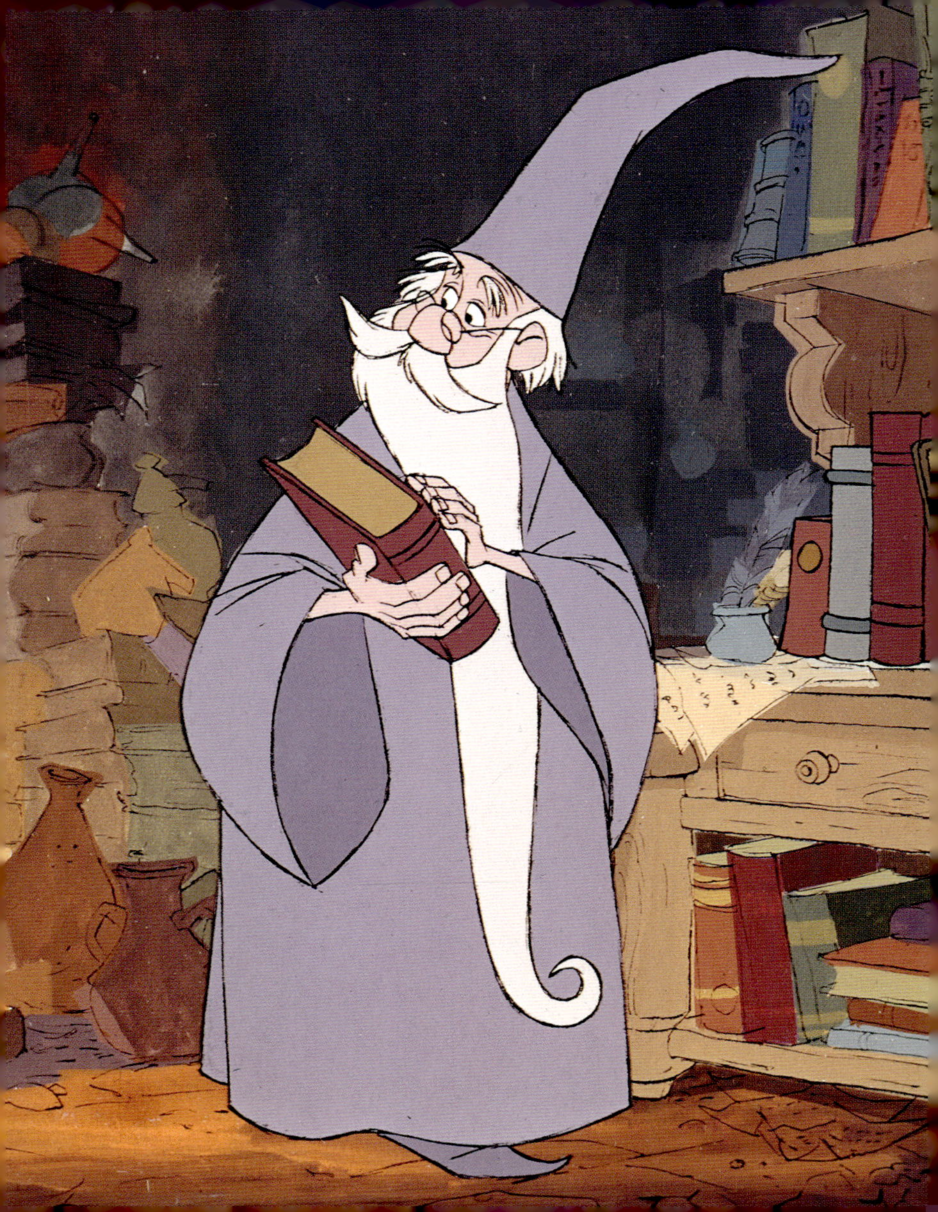

I trust in the goodness of others.

✦

Love is stronger than gravity. This mighty force can strengthen and weaken us, make us smile or cry, and attract us to each other. But with such power comes responsibility. Treat those you love with care and wisdom.

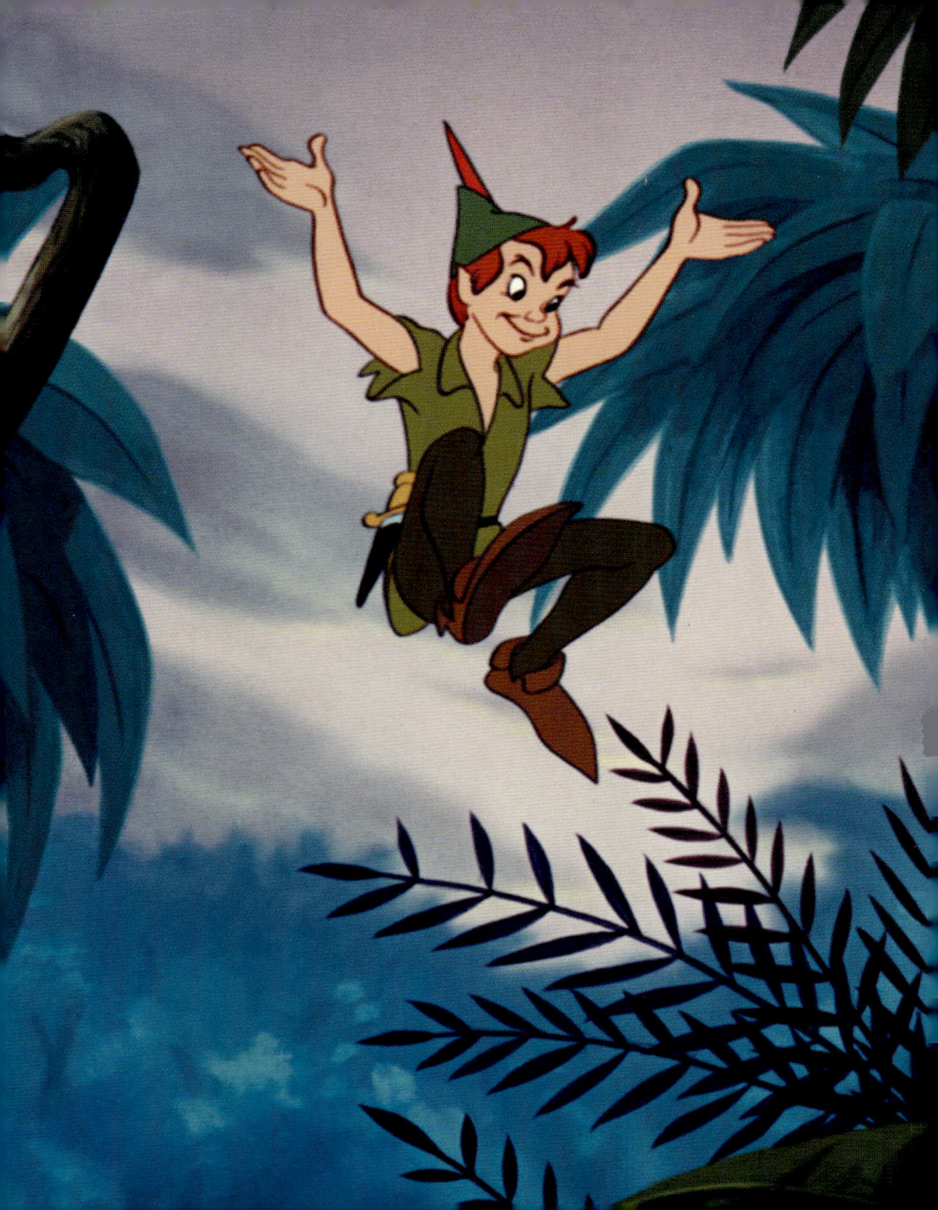

I think happy thoughts.

★

Negative thoughts weigh heavy on our hearts and minds, and anchor us to the ground. Free your positive side. Say "I can!" and fly... Second star to the right and straight on till morning.

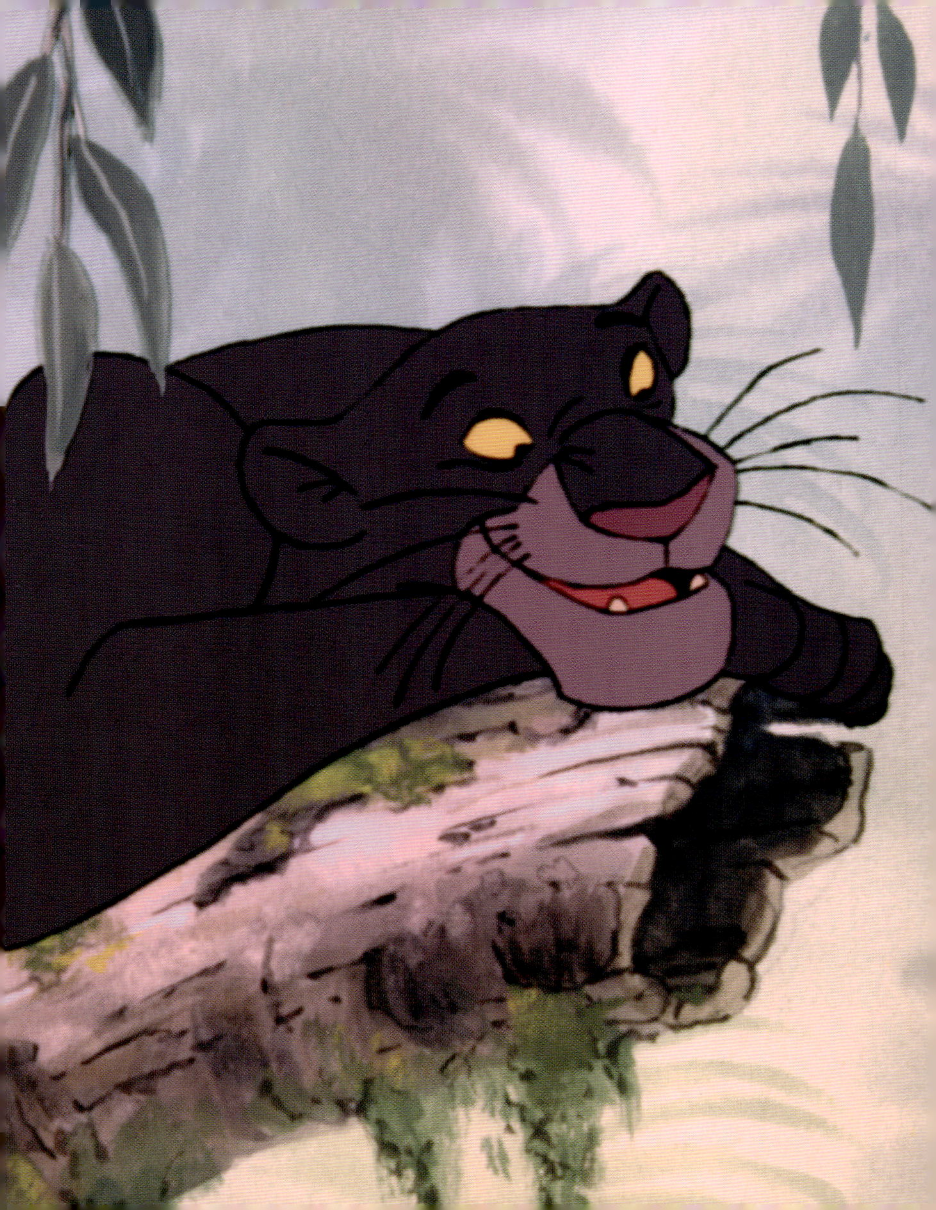

Each new
day is a chance to
begin again.

★

When you're angry, sad or
afraid, don't be too hasty
in your words and actions.
Give yourself some time, and
breathe deeply. After a good
night's sleep, you might find
that things aren't as bad
as they seemed.

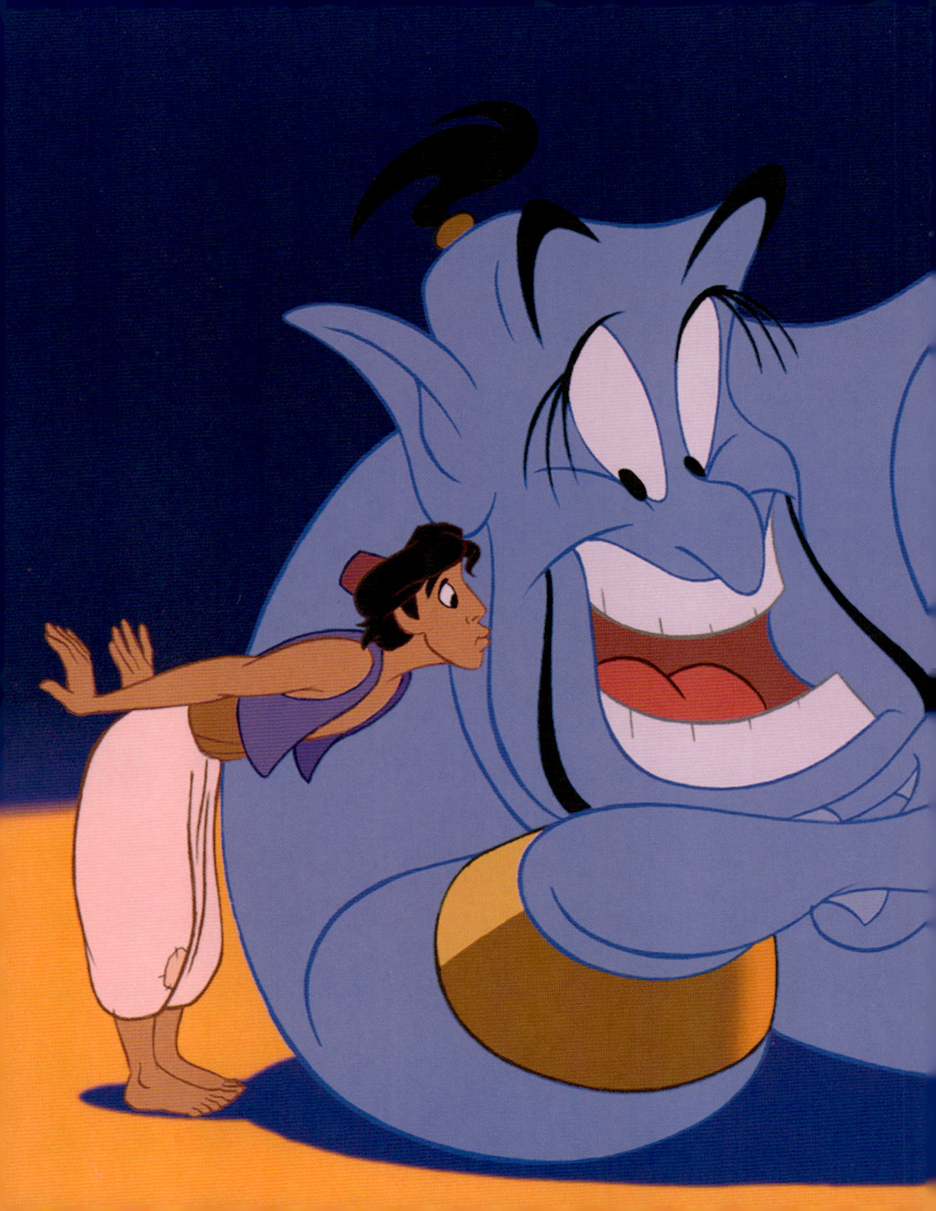

I am curious.

★

Even if you're on a magic carpet, hearing only yourself talk can get pretty dull. Be curious about other people. Give them space to express themselves. Listen. Others will like you more, and you might learn something new.

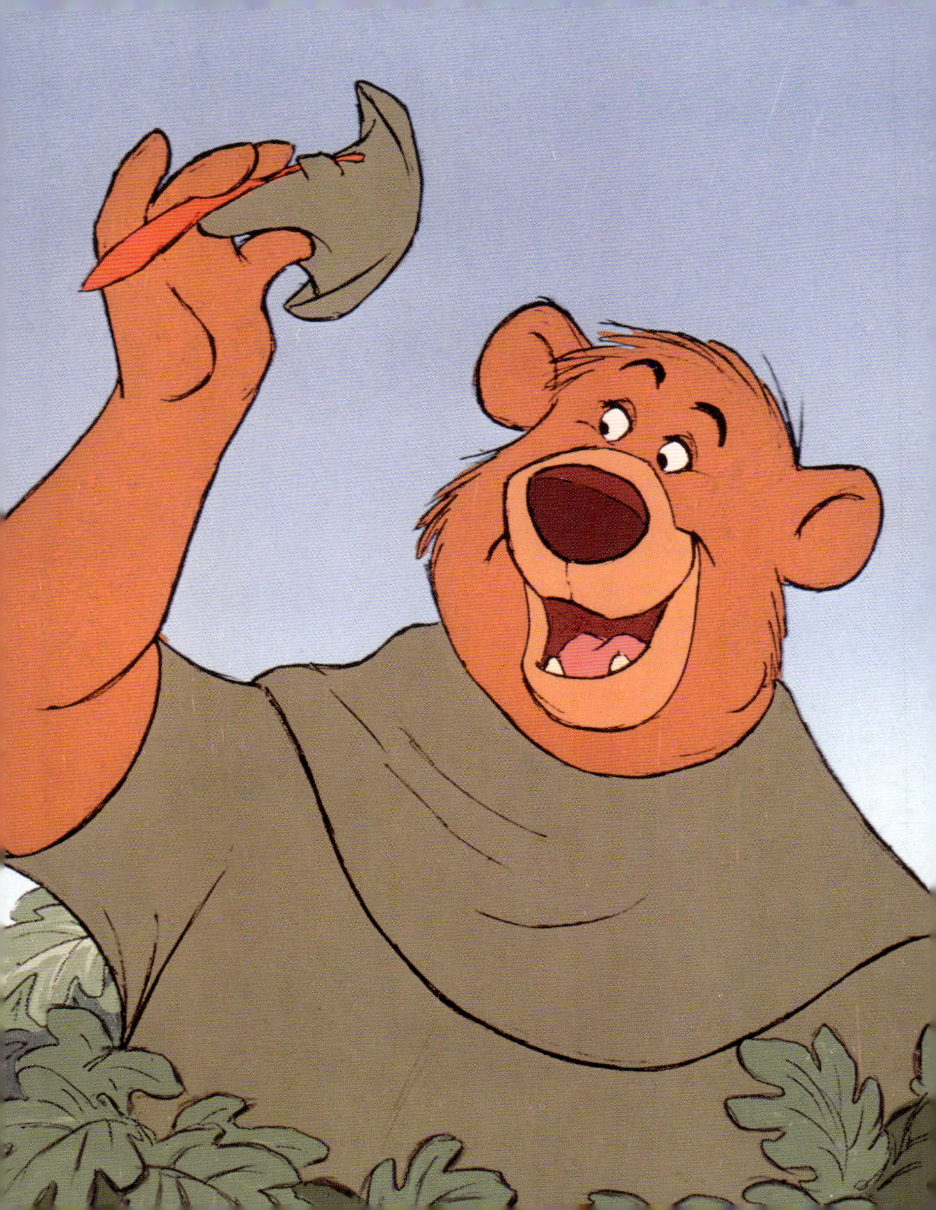

I believe in doing good and I am true to myself.

★

Reality is often more complex than it appears. No one is perfect. But if you identify your true values and use them as a compass, it will be easier to find your way through the forest.

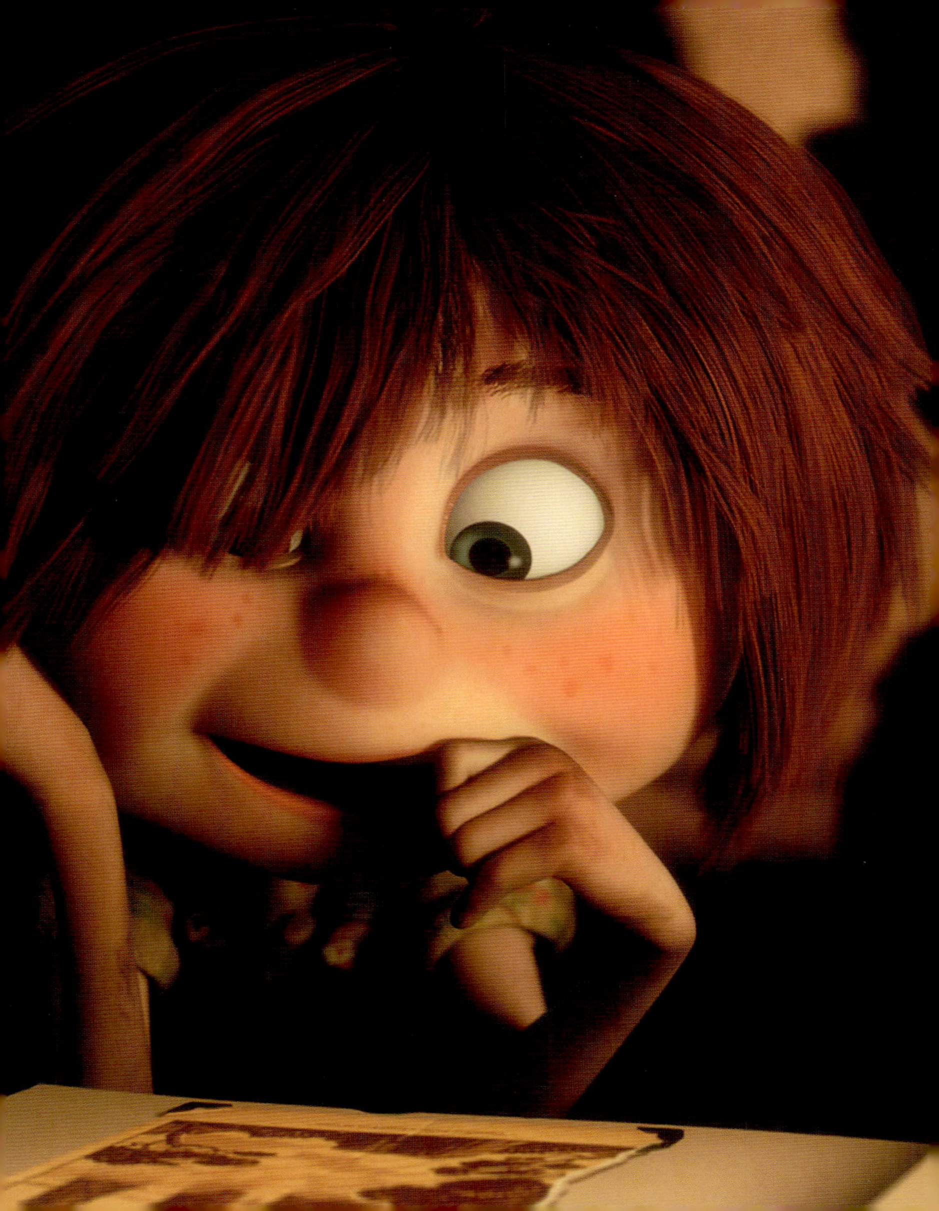

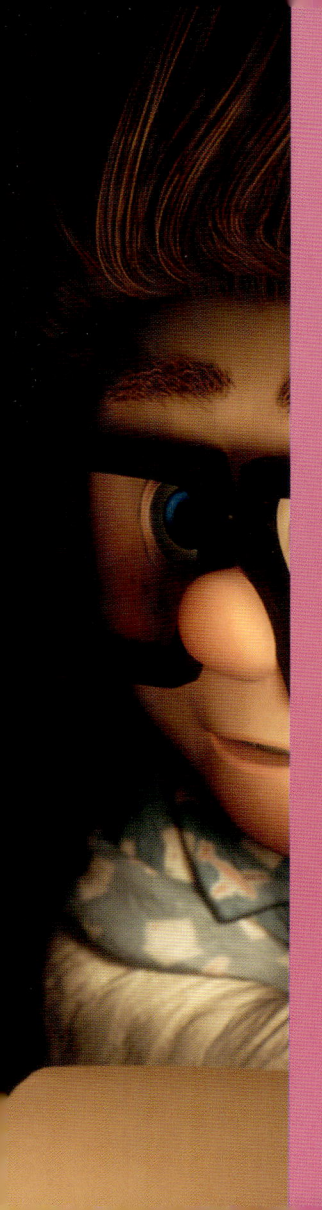

My past has prepared me for my future.

★

Appreciate those who accompany you on your journey, and try to be ready to say goodbye and move on. The memories of the past should not hold you back from flying.

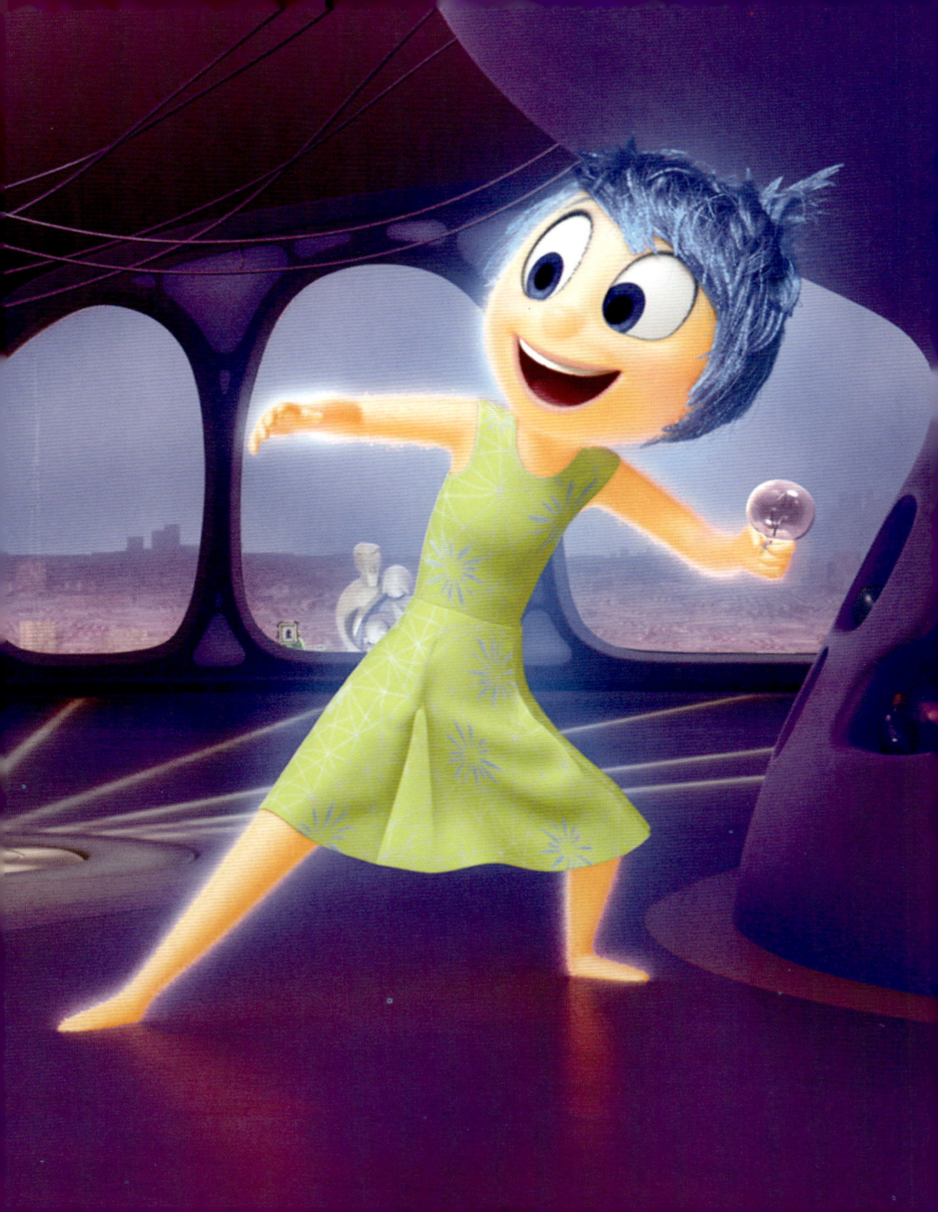

I am open to feeling all my emotions.

★

Embrace life's balance of beauty and ugliness, happiness and pain. Without sadness, there would be no joy. Every experience is a part of who we are.

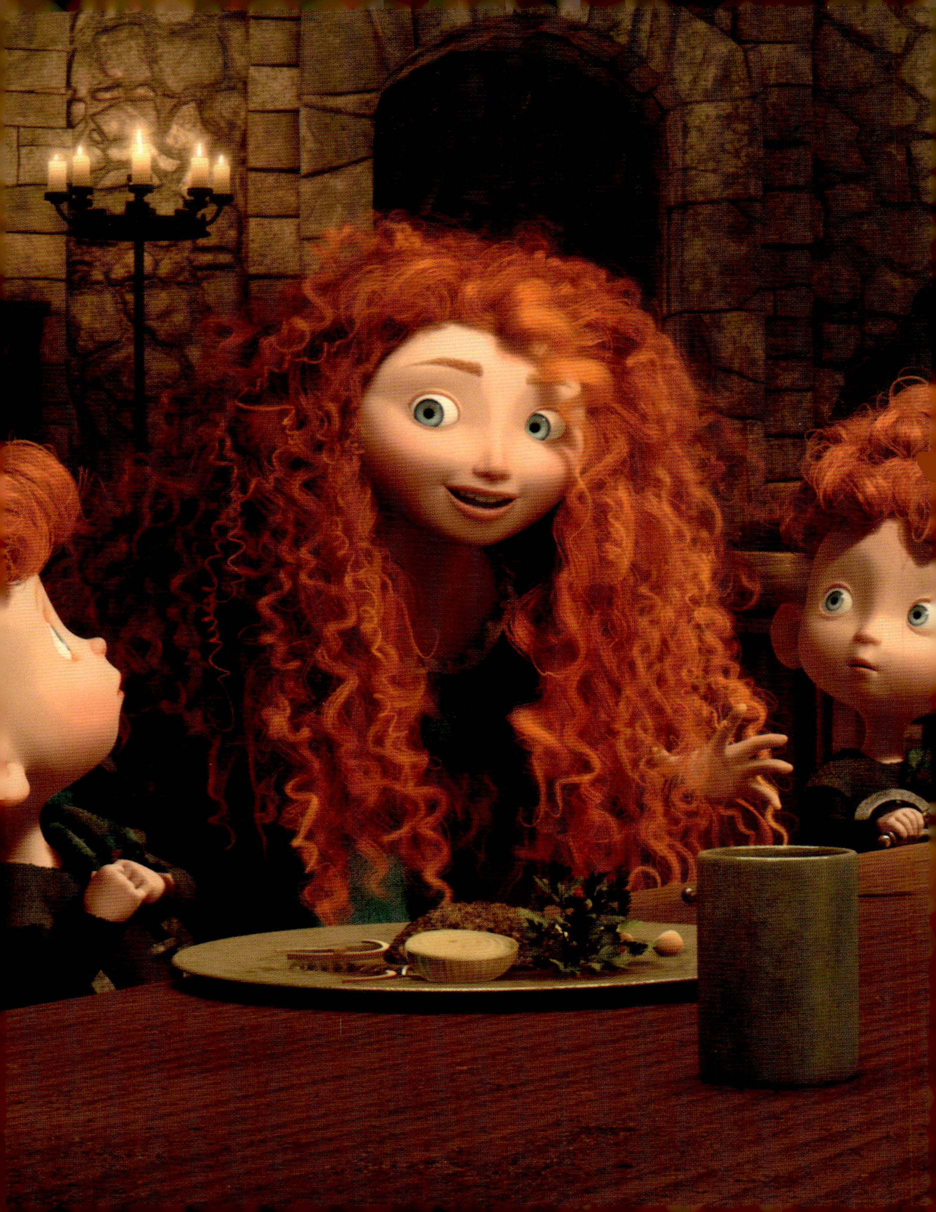

My relationships are important to me.

★

The delicate fabric of human relationships is woven over time. If pride creates a tear, take a needle and humbly work to mend the rift.

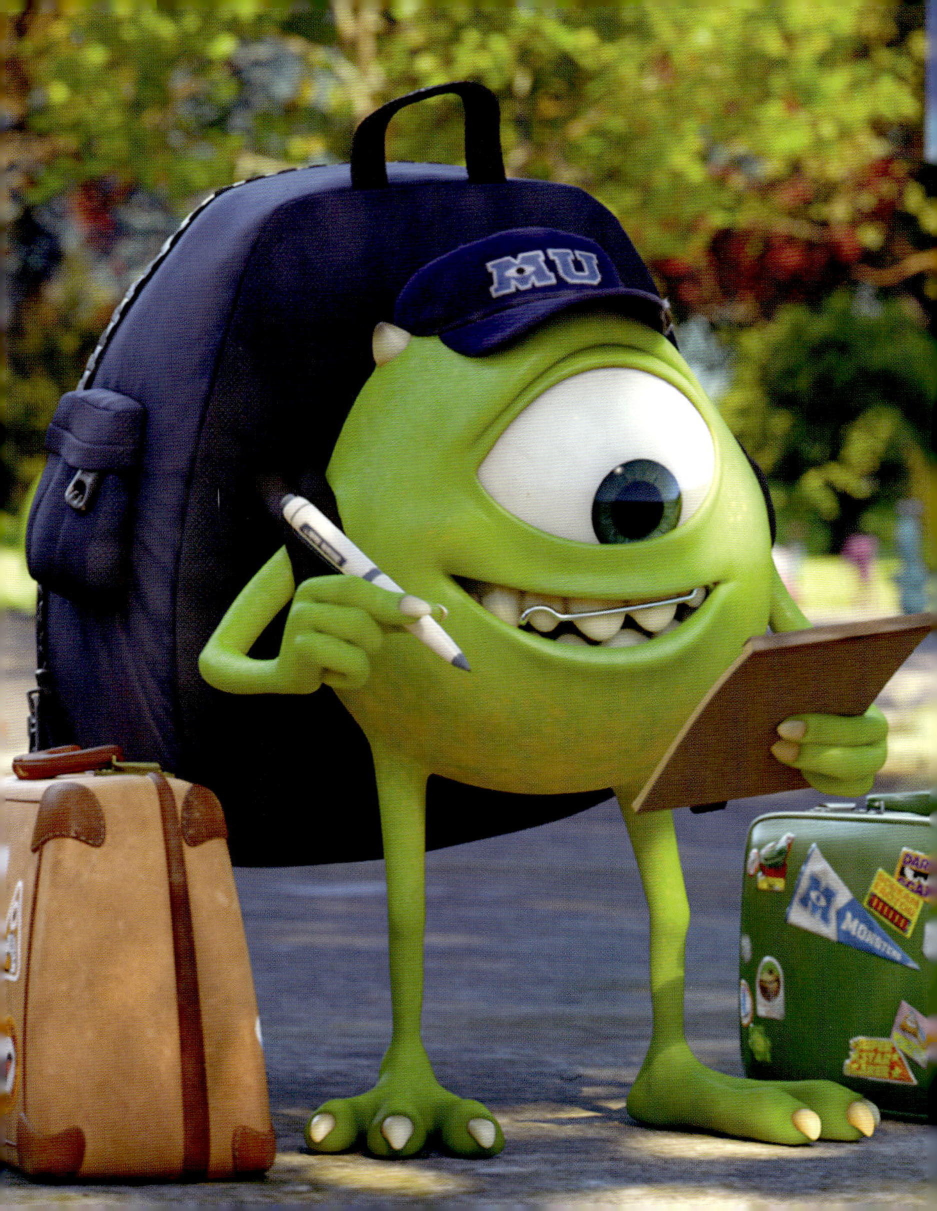
MU

I welcome the experience of failure.

★

Sometimes we have to face our own limits. Failure can be painful, but it can help us to grow. Take a new path. Pursue a new dream.

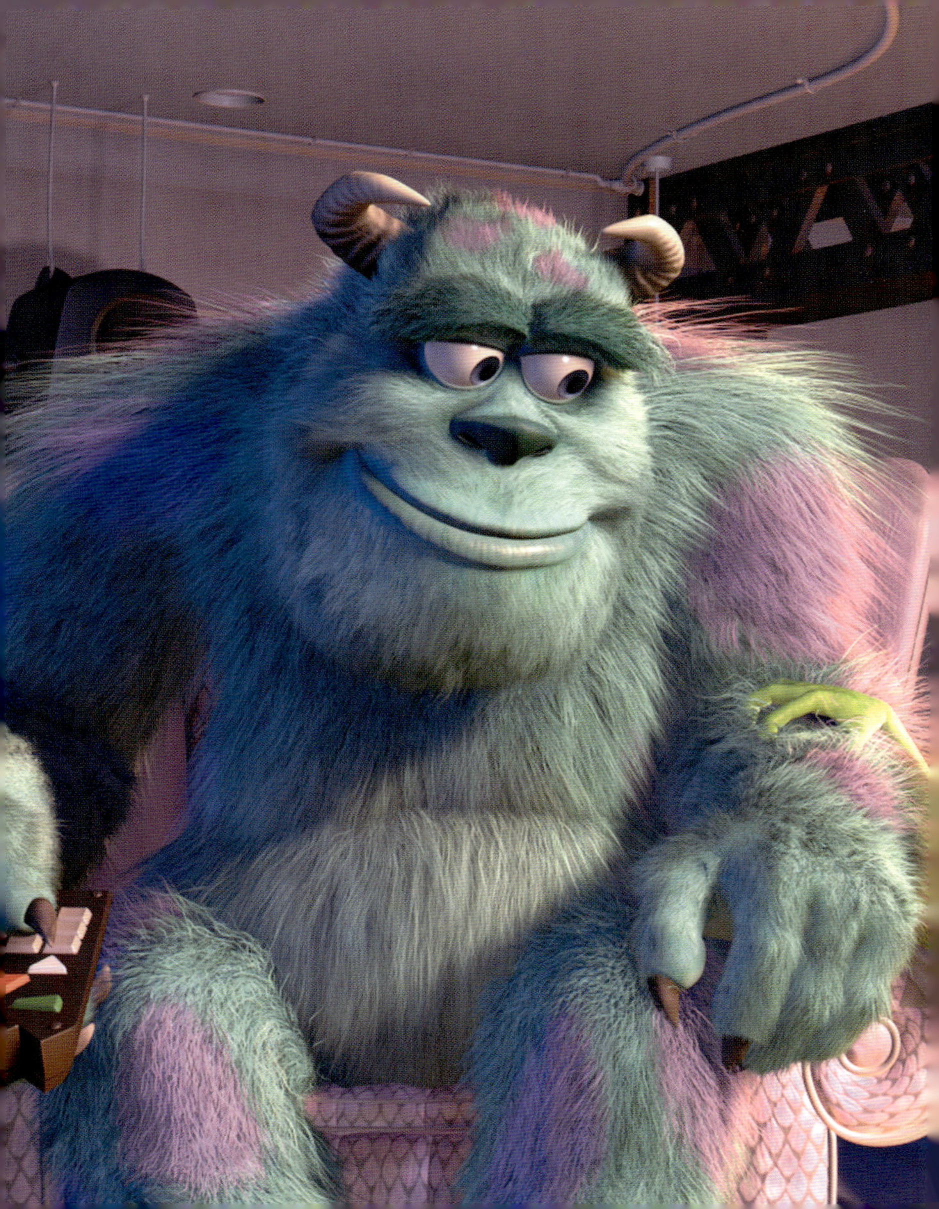

I am not afraid to laugh loudly.

★

In relationships, we both generate and absorb energy. Our words and actions can have a positive or negative impact. So remember: laughter generates better energy than fear.

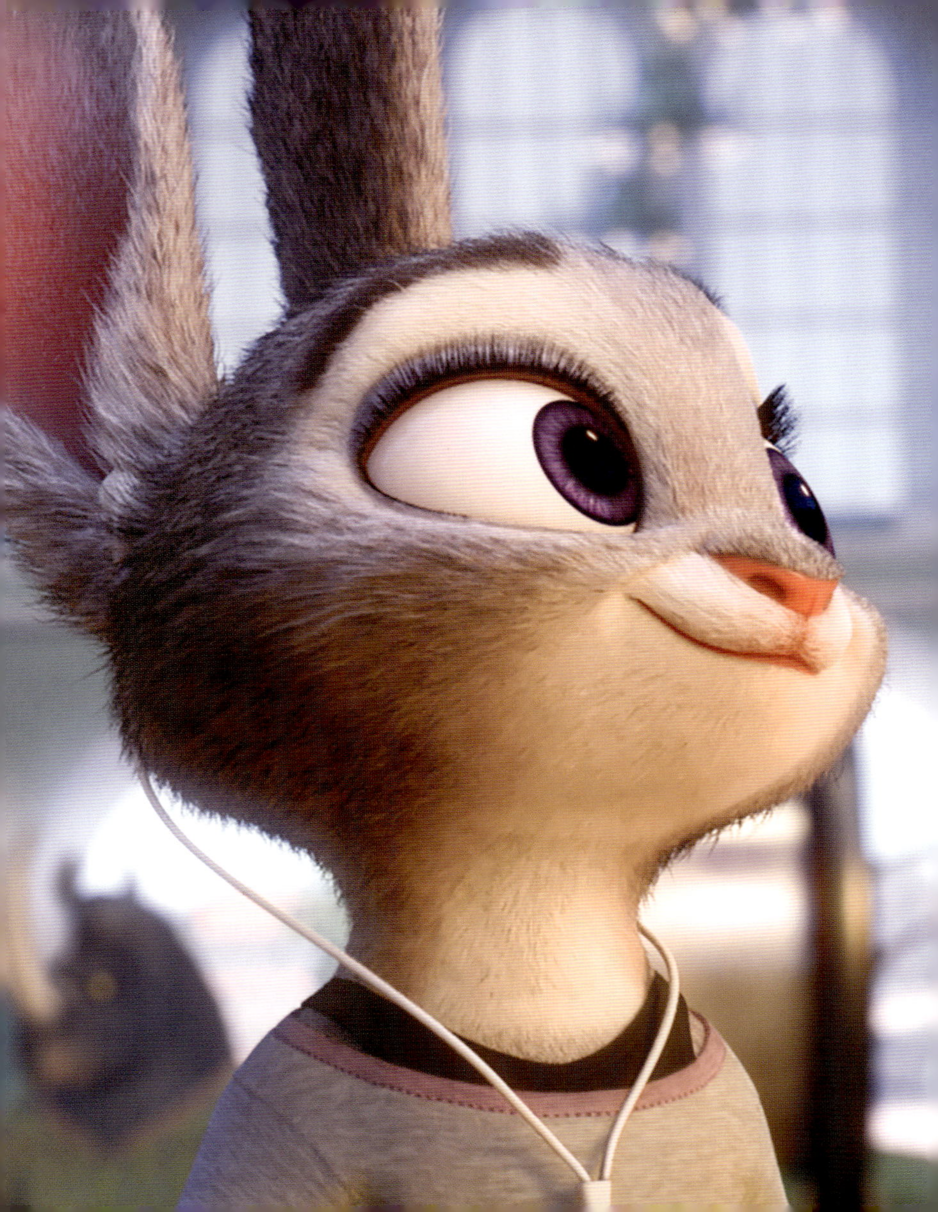

I am safe and surrounded by people who understand me.

★

Empathy fosters respect, trust and connection. A community built on empathy is a place where everyone is free to be their true self.

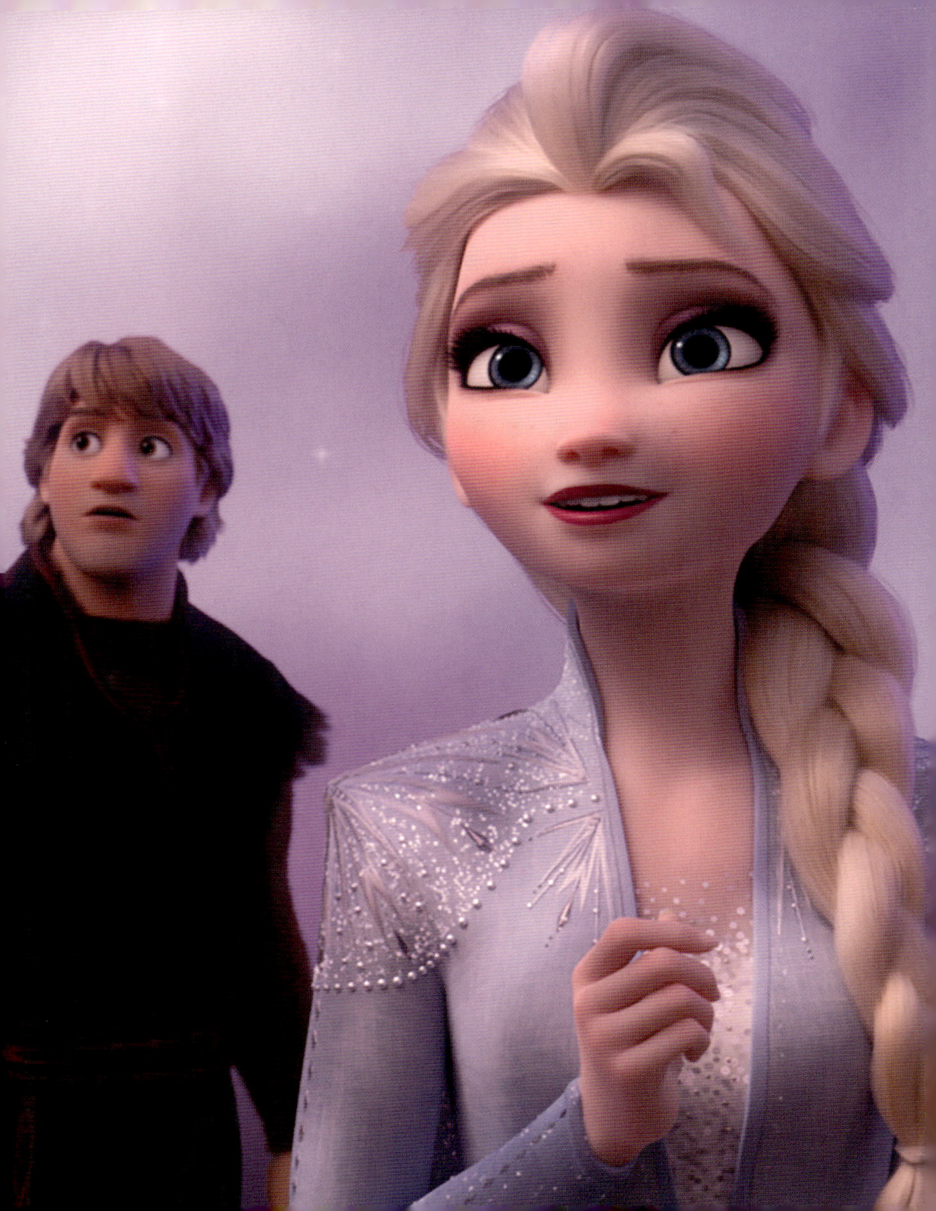

I am not afraid to be myself.

★

Nobody's perfect. Accept and take pride in who you are. Whatever storms come your way, believe in yourself and trust that you will find your unique path in life.

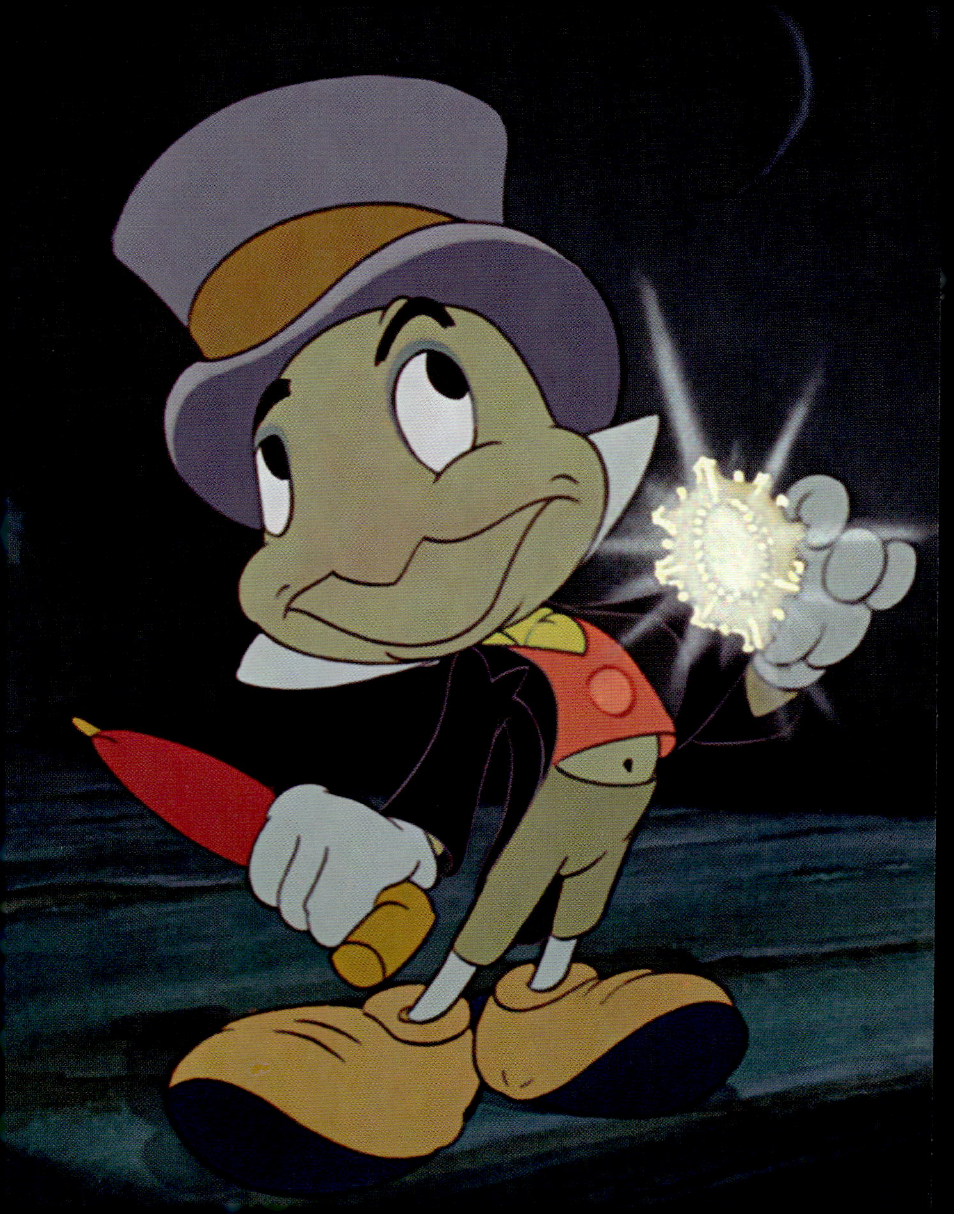

I trust myself.

★

Whether your inner voice is crashing your party or feeding your wild side, listen to it carefully. Your conscience is a vital navigational tool to help you find balance between responsibility and recklessness.

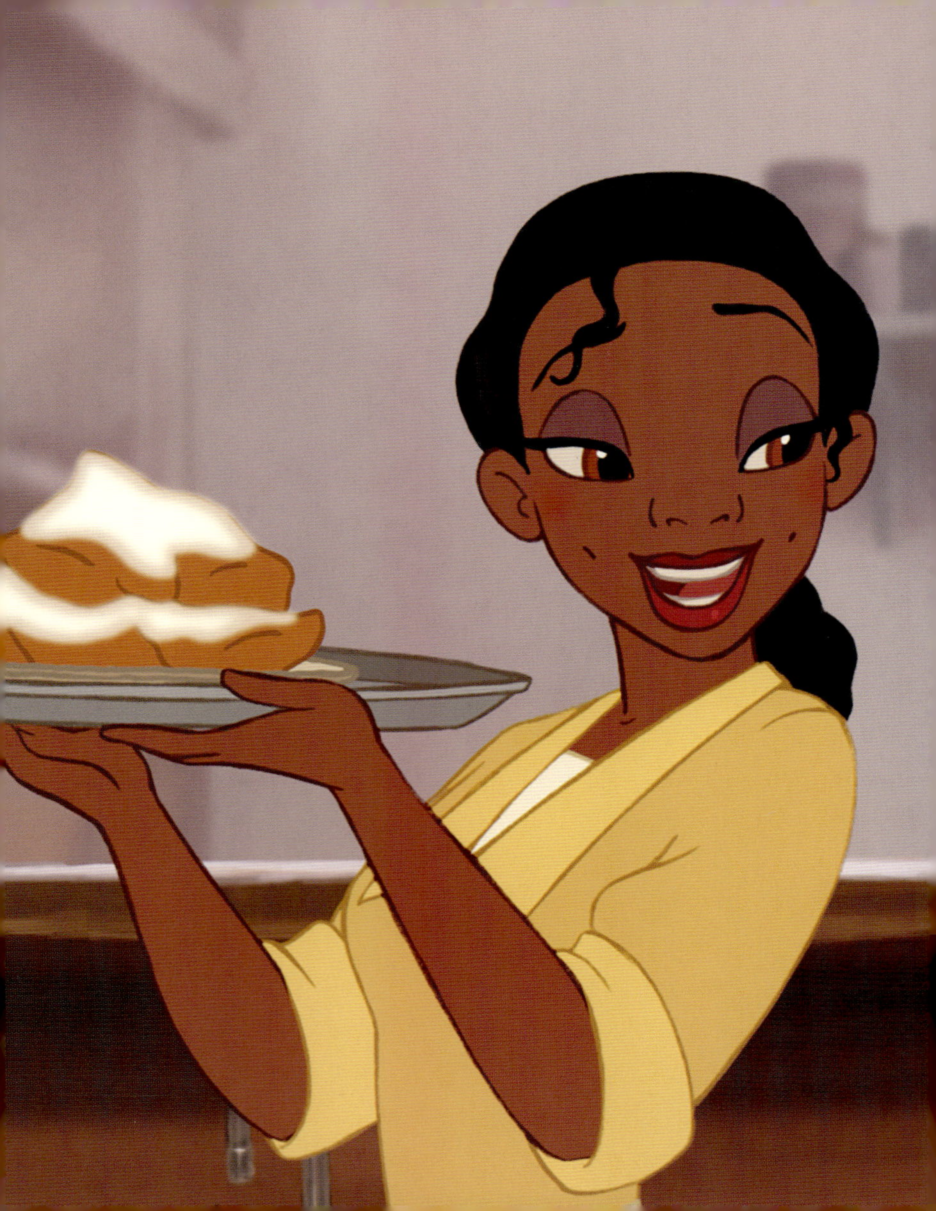

I work hard and deserve success.

★

Beyond the sun, sky and sea, little comes for free in this life. Tired muscles and the gratification of a challenge completed are the surest route to satisfaction and success.

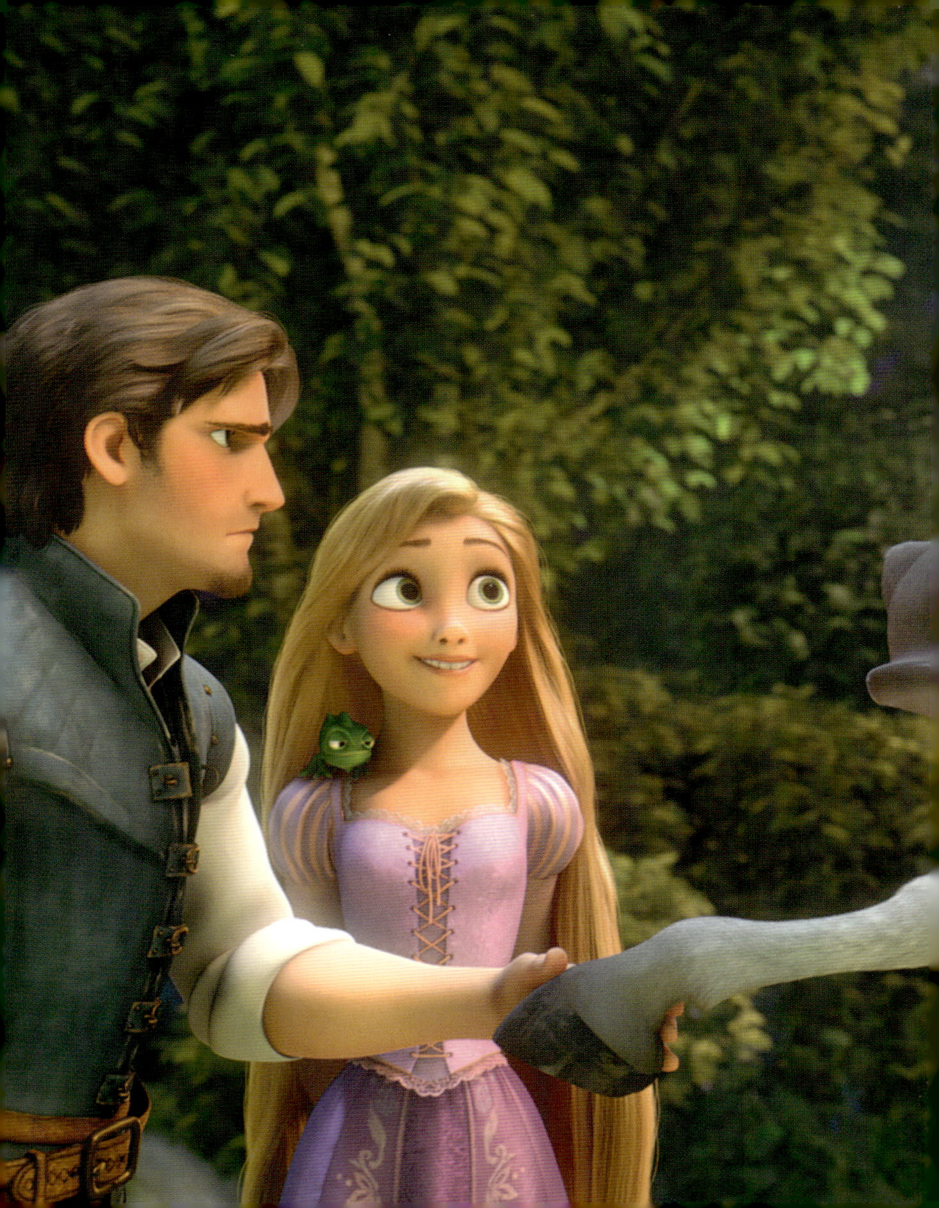

I am adventurous.

✶

Fear of disappointment can paralyse you. Standing still is safe, but it won't get you anywhere. Live life to the fullest. Step into the unknown.

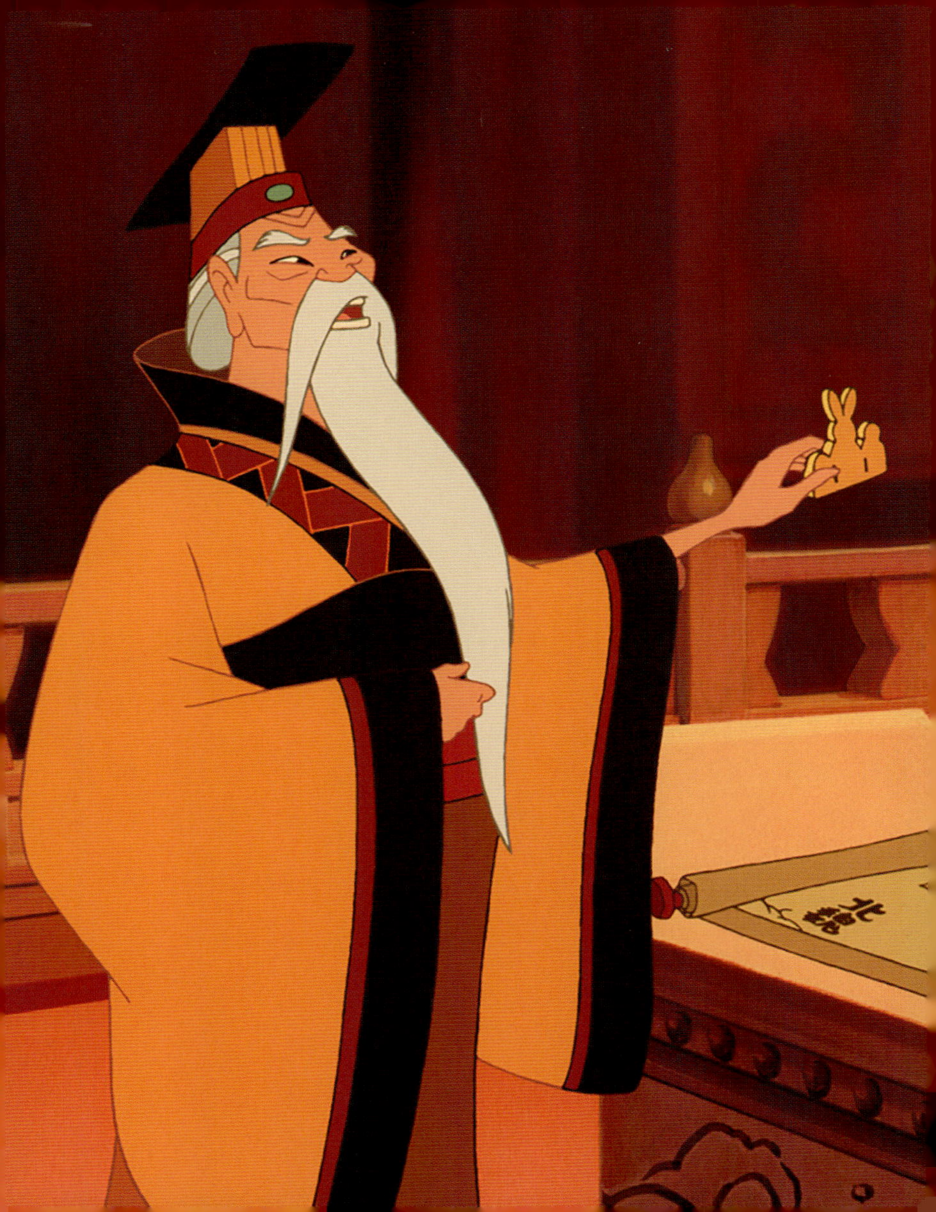

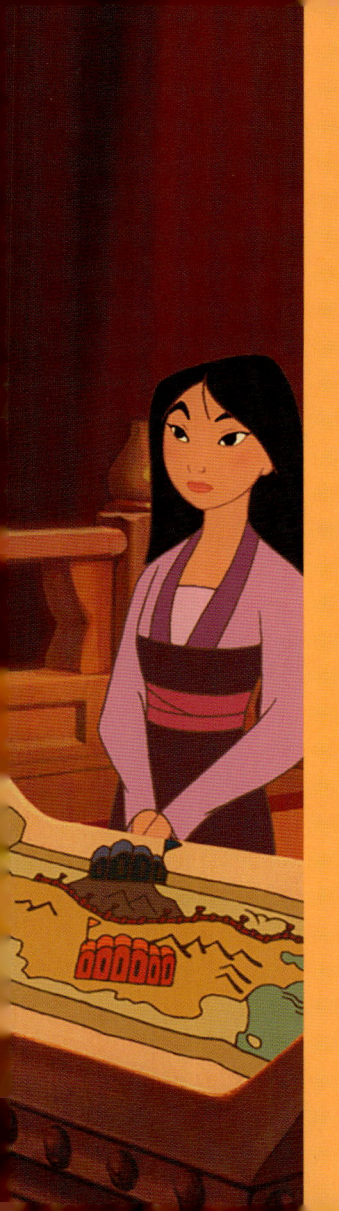

I am resilient.

✶

Sometimes our resilience is tested by droughts, storms or darkness. However, these difficult times may teach us valuable lessons about ourselves and others. With every challenge overcome, you will grow stronger and bloom more beautifully.

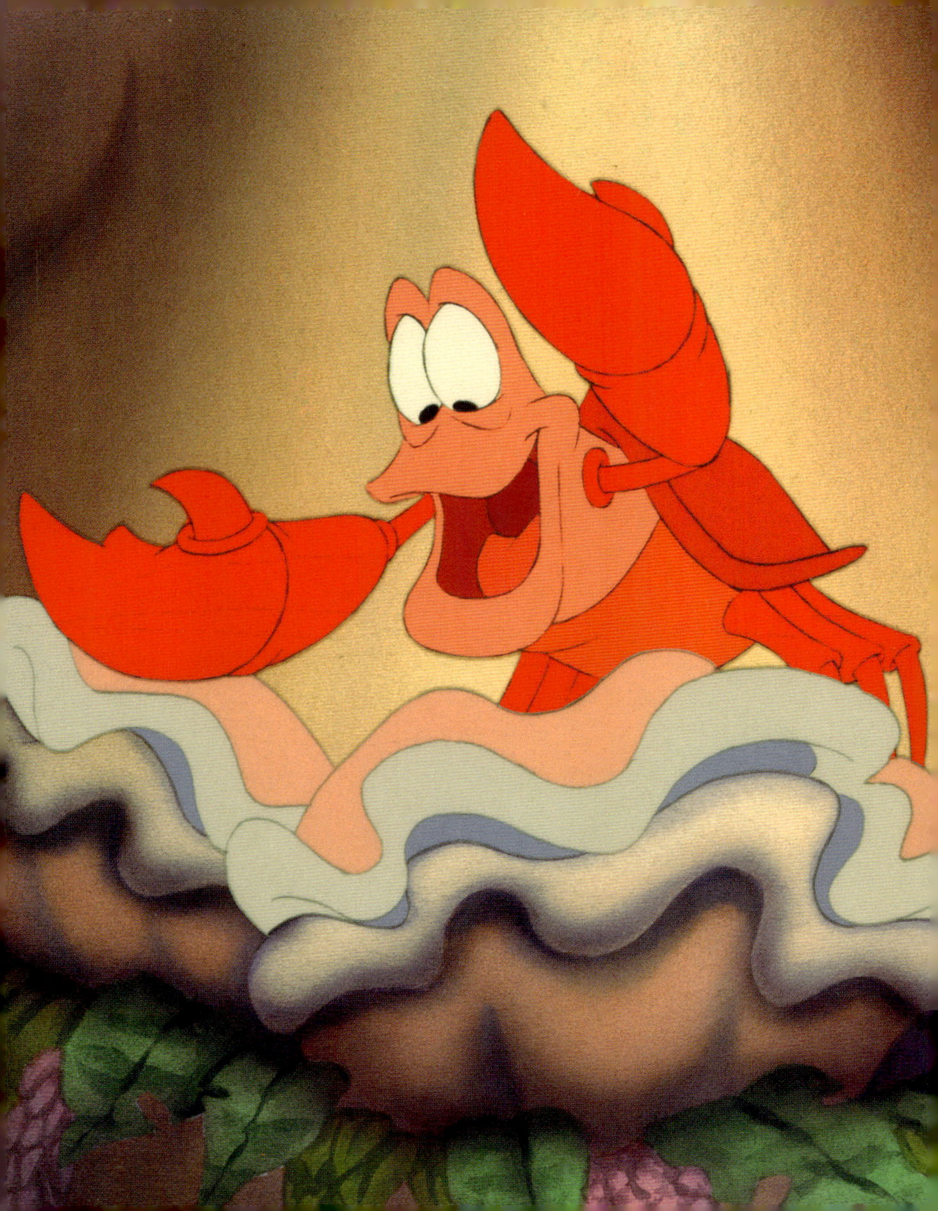

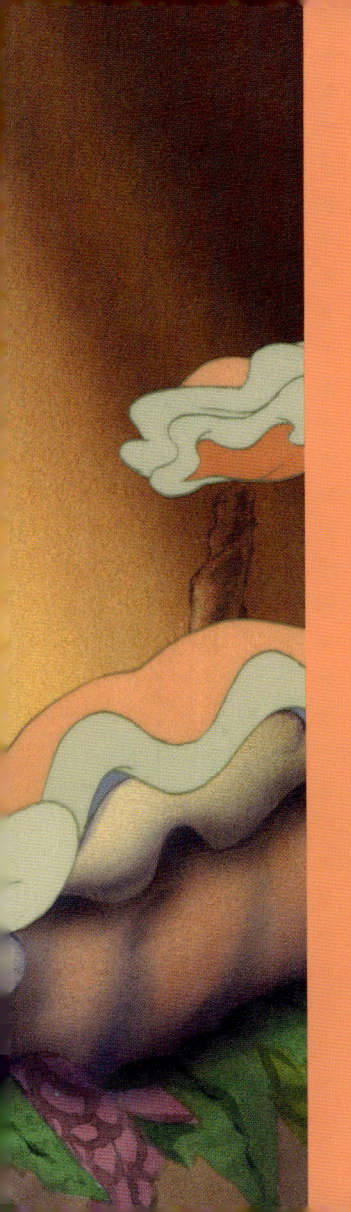

I am a supportive friend.

★

Our first reactions often reflect our own limited points of view, rather than what is best in that situation. Sometimes it is better to stand back, listen and simply support our loved ones in accomplishing their own dreams.

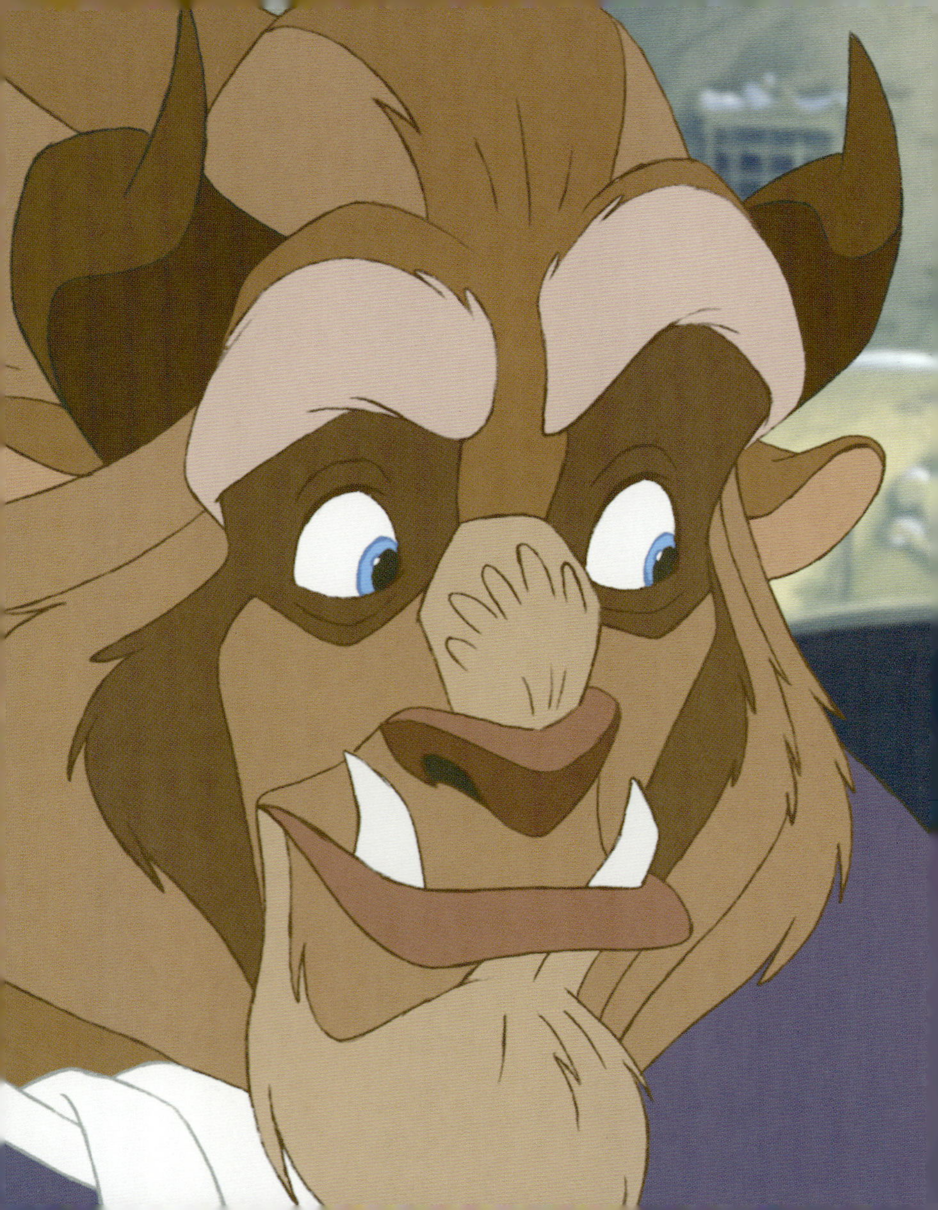

What is meant for me will find me.

★

To love is not to own. It means choosing freely to share a path. Letting go of the other's hand may be a risk, but only by doing so can you be sure that you truly belong together.

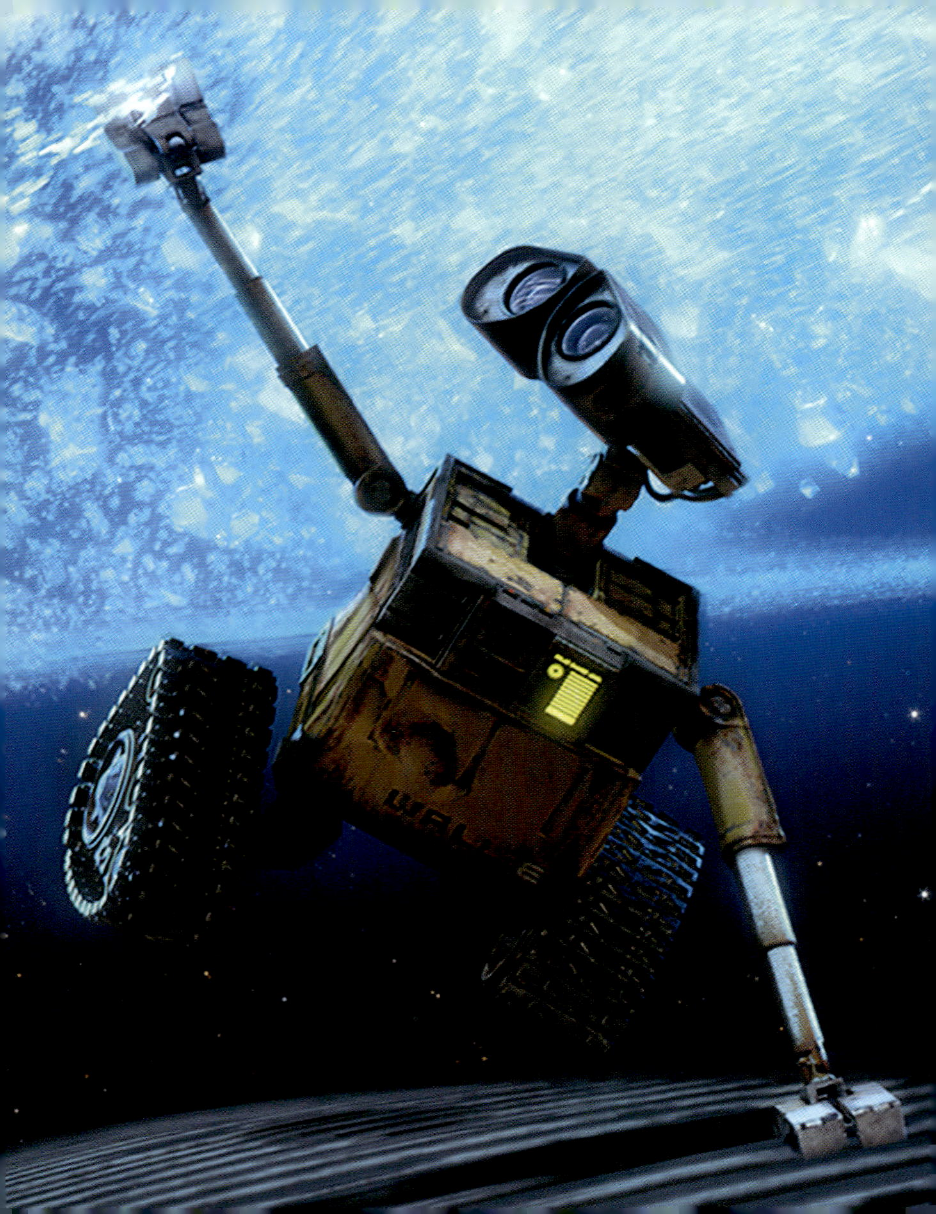

I am not afraid to express myself.

★

If you can't say the words, find another way. Turn on a piece of music, dance and express what your heart truly feels.

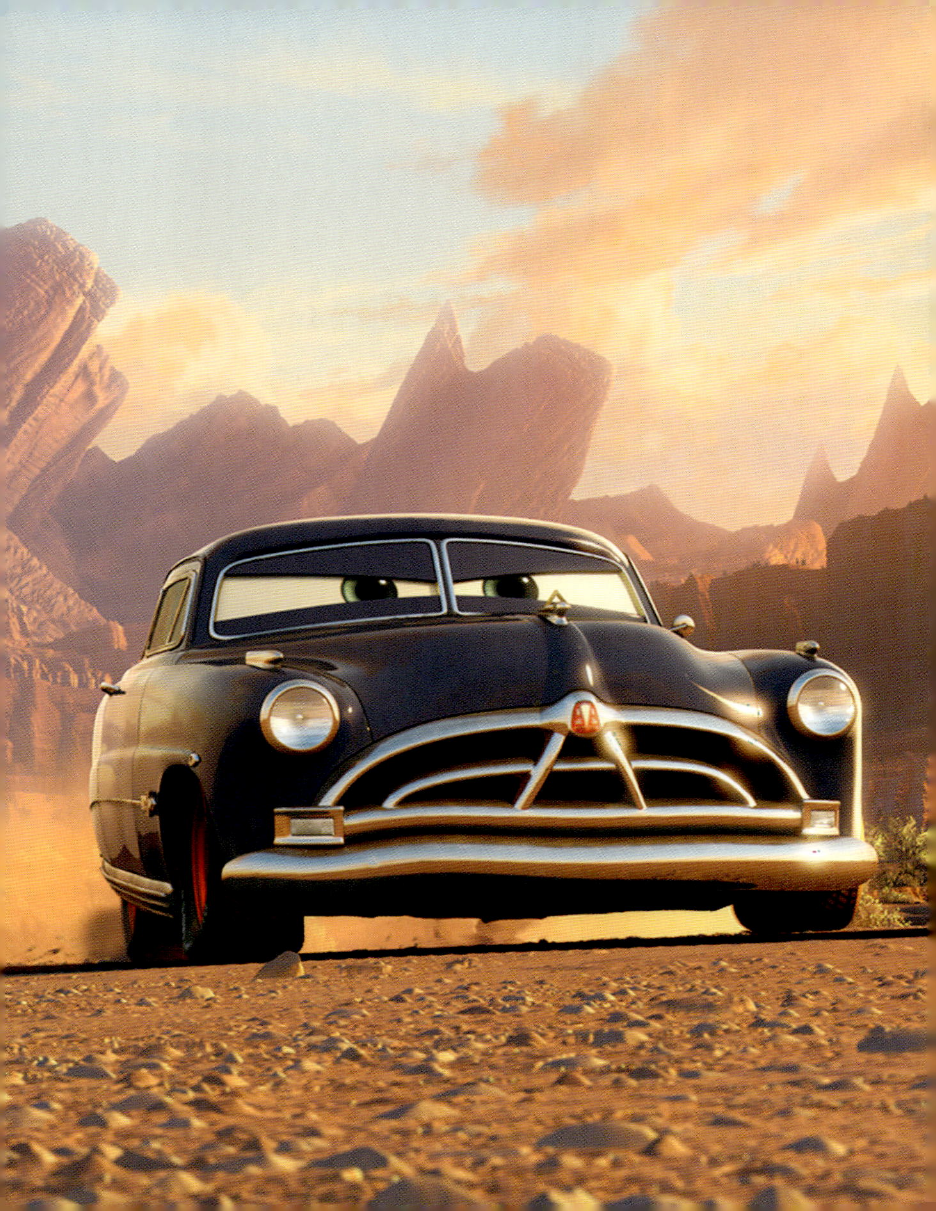

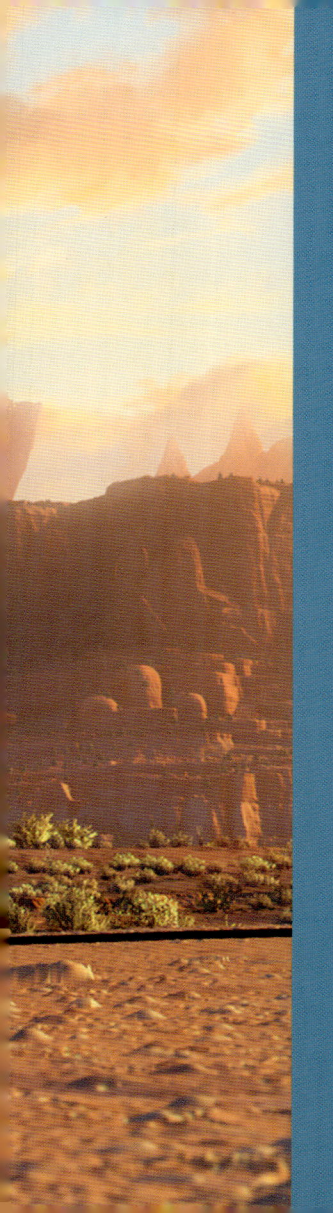

I choose my own path.

★

Rejecting the conventional route is sometimes the only way to make progress. When you feel stuck, try turning strongly left in order to go right.

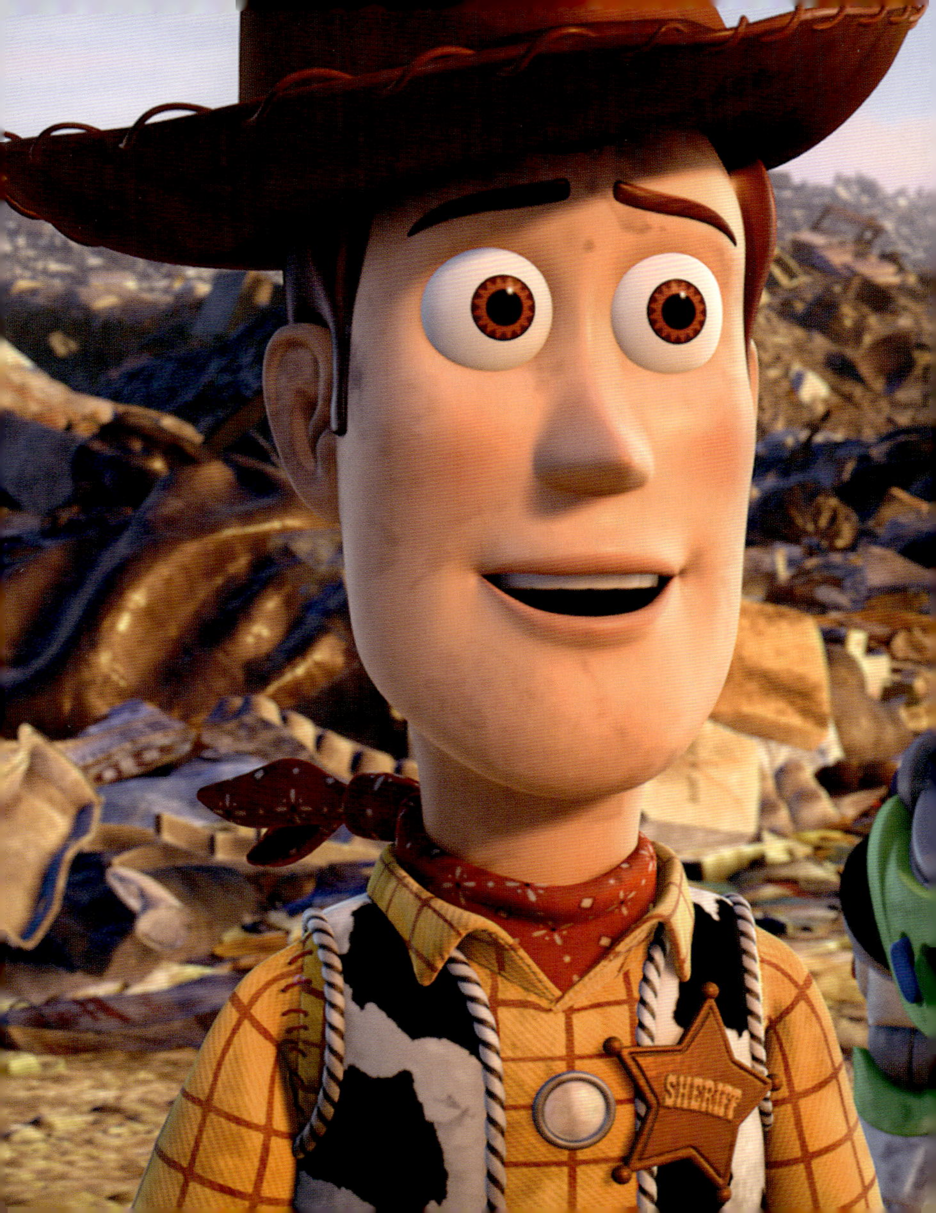
SHERIFF

I am flexible and open to change.

★

However much we try to resist, things in life will keep changing. Embrace the new opportunities, adapt and remember: if you want to change the world, you also have to change with the world.

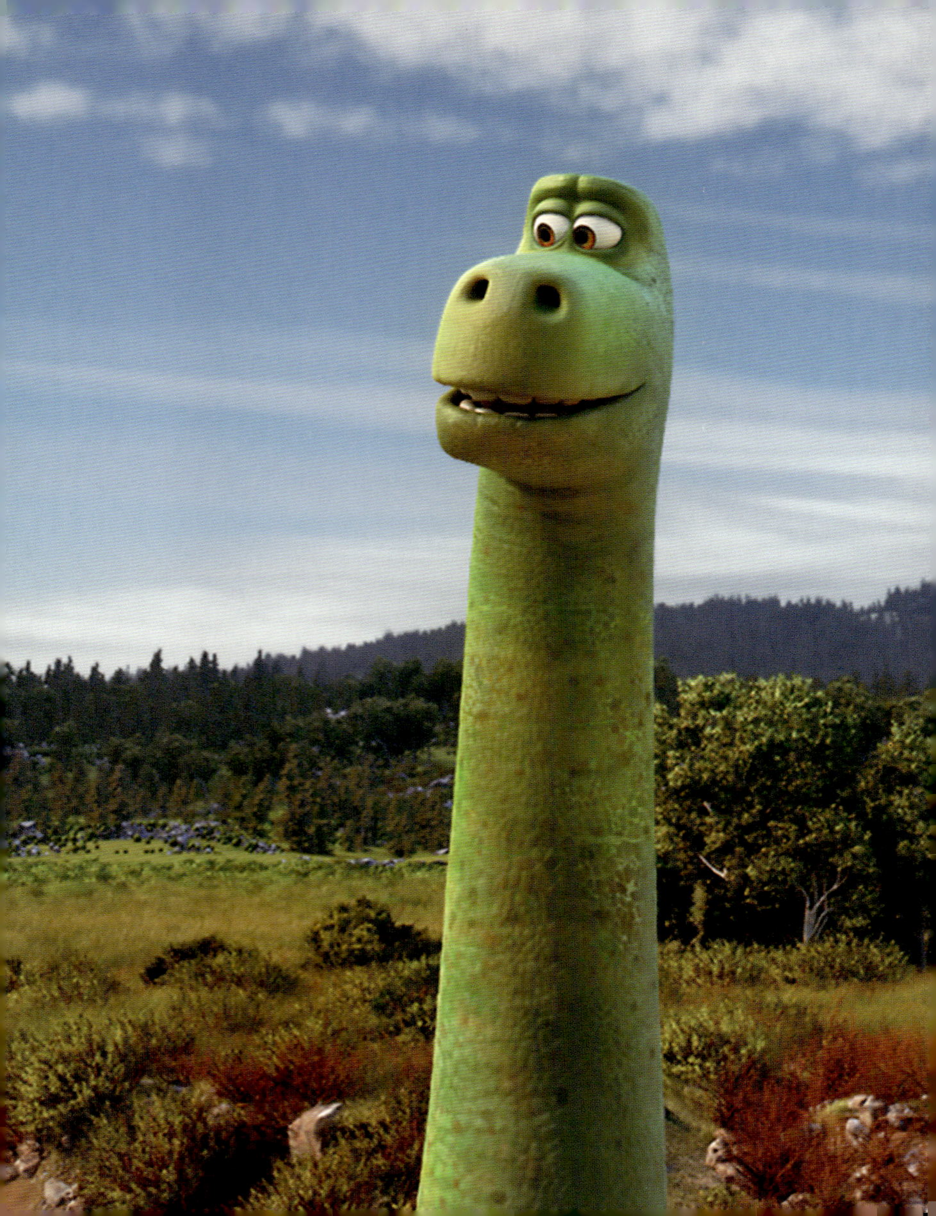

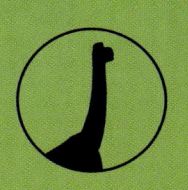

I can do hard things.

★

Overcoming our fears is the first step toward fully realising our potential. Only by welcoming the darkness can we finally play among the stars... and fireflies.

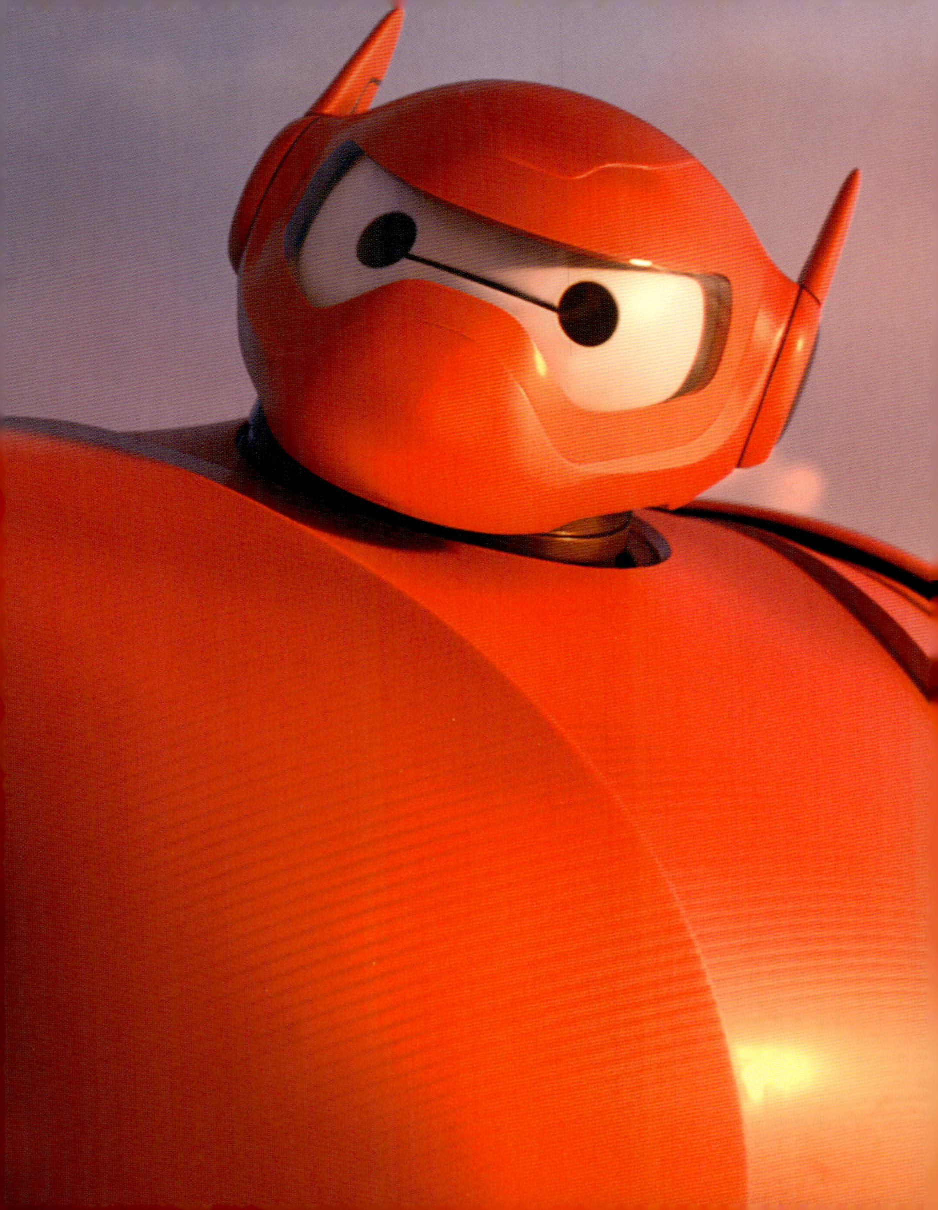

Asking for help is a sign of strength.

★

Don't be afraid to look vulnerable. Learn to ask for help, and to accept it from others. The ability to connect to others emotionally is a superpower.

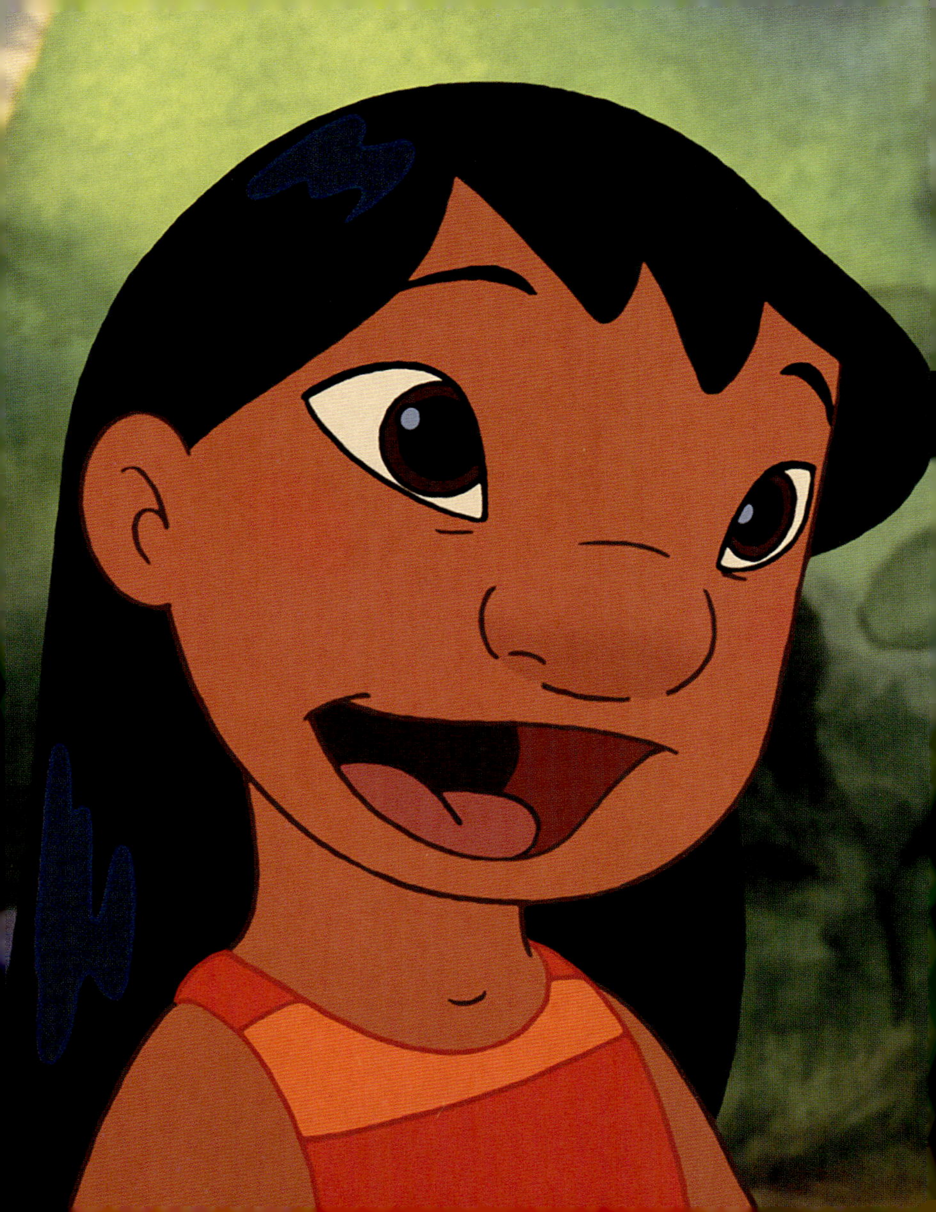

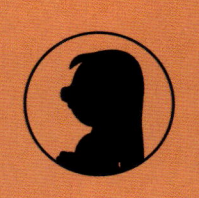

I share my life with others.

★

We all need attention: celebration for our successes, support for our failures, and encouragement to overcome our fears. Recognise the value of others, and they will recognise yours.

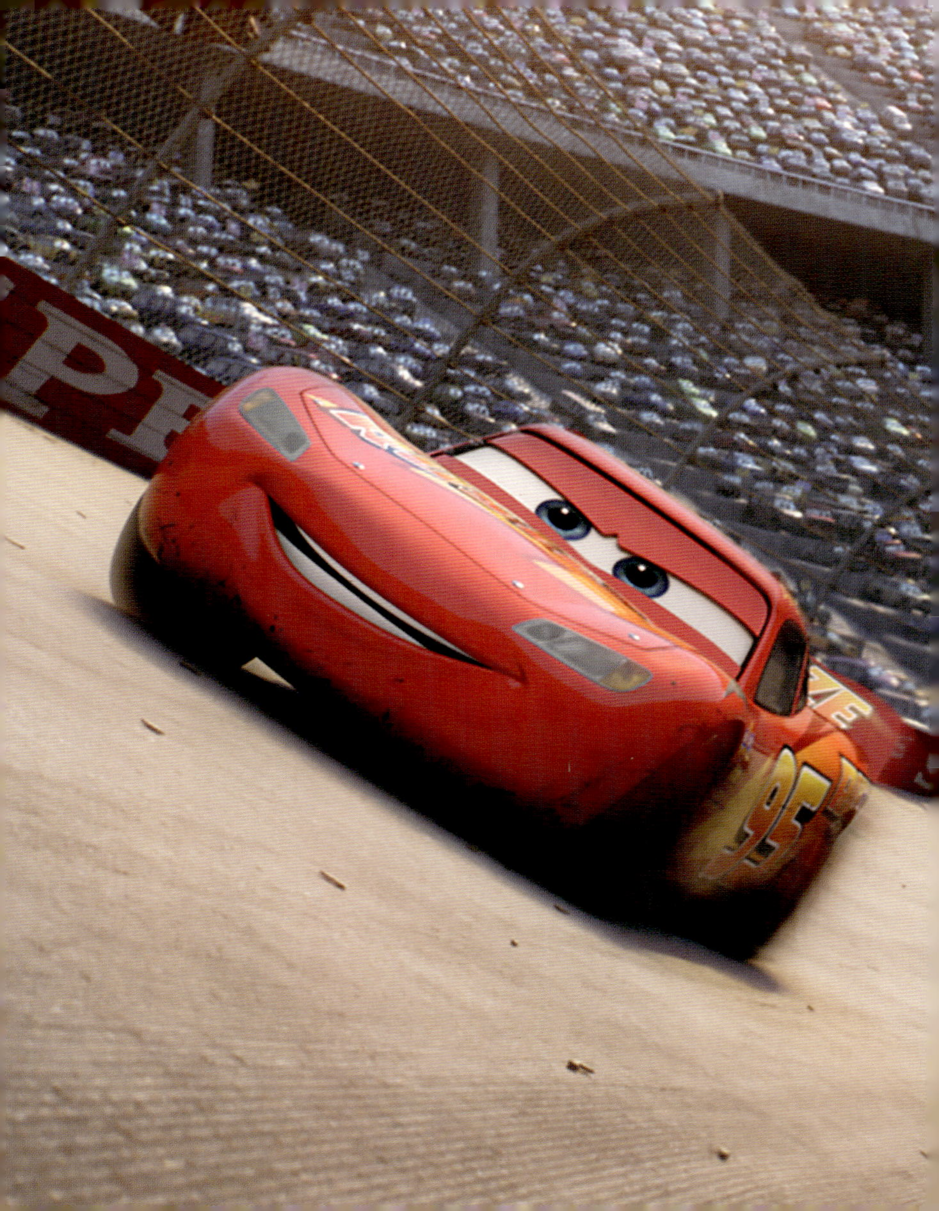
95

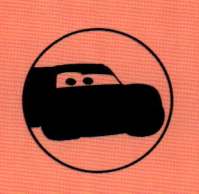

I take the steps
I need to achieve
my goals.

★

New problems can't be
solved using old solutions.
Remember your true goal,
and then ask yourself:
which new road can I
take to achieve it?

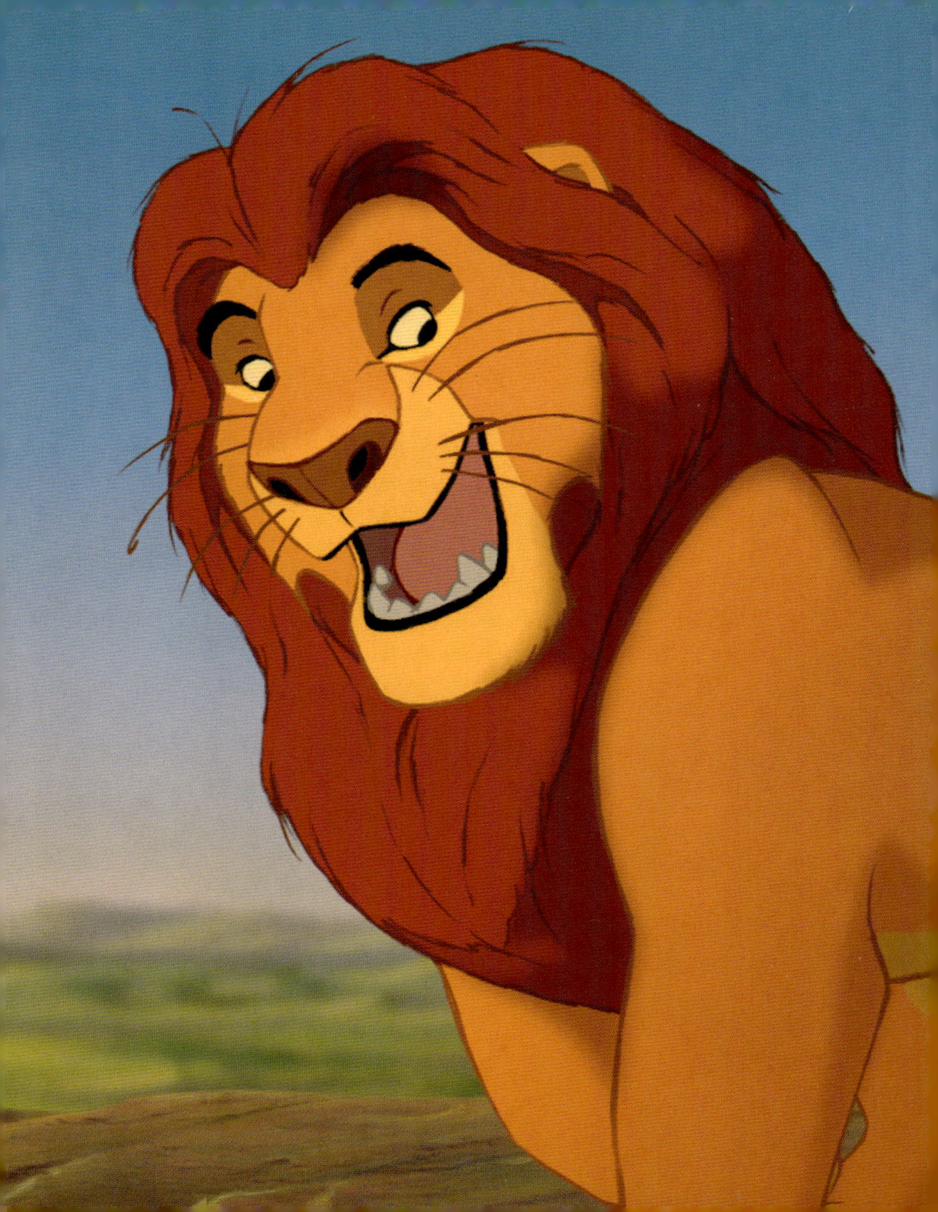

I strive for balance in my life.

★

A successful community depends on a balance between private instinct and collective interest. Understanding and respecting this balance is the key to everybody's well-being.

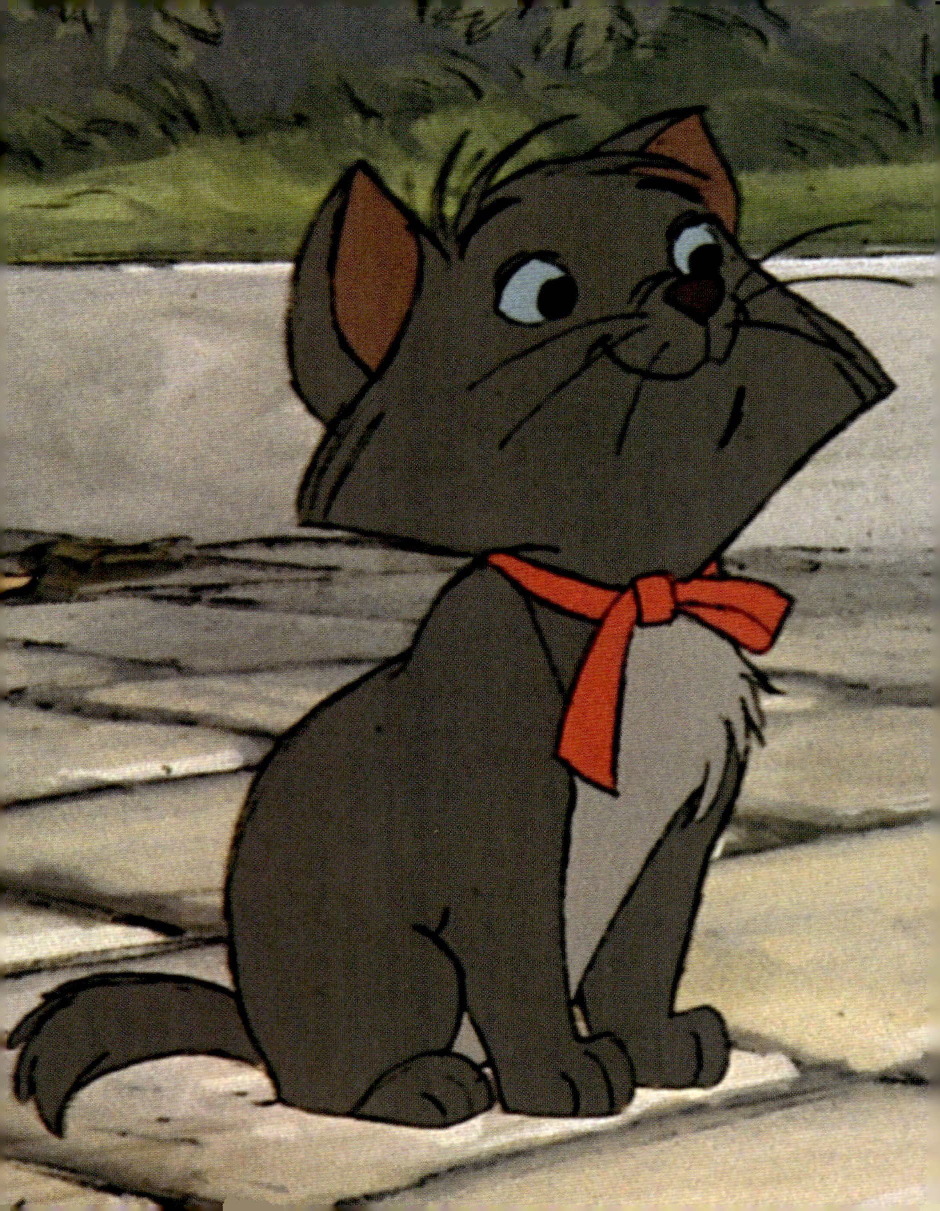

I am one of a kind.

★

Draw inspiration from the
great masters, but find your
distinctive way to leave a
mark. Greatness is often
remembered for
its originality.

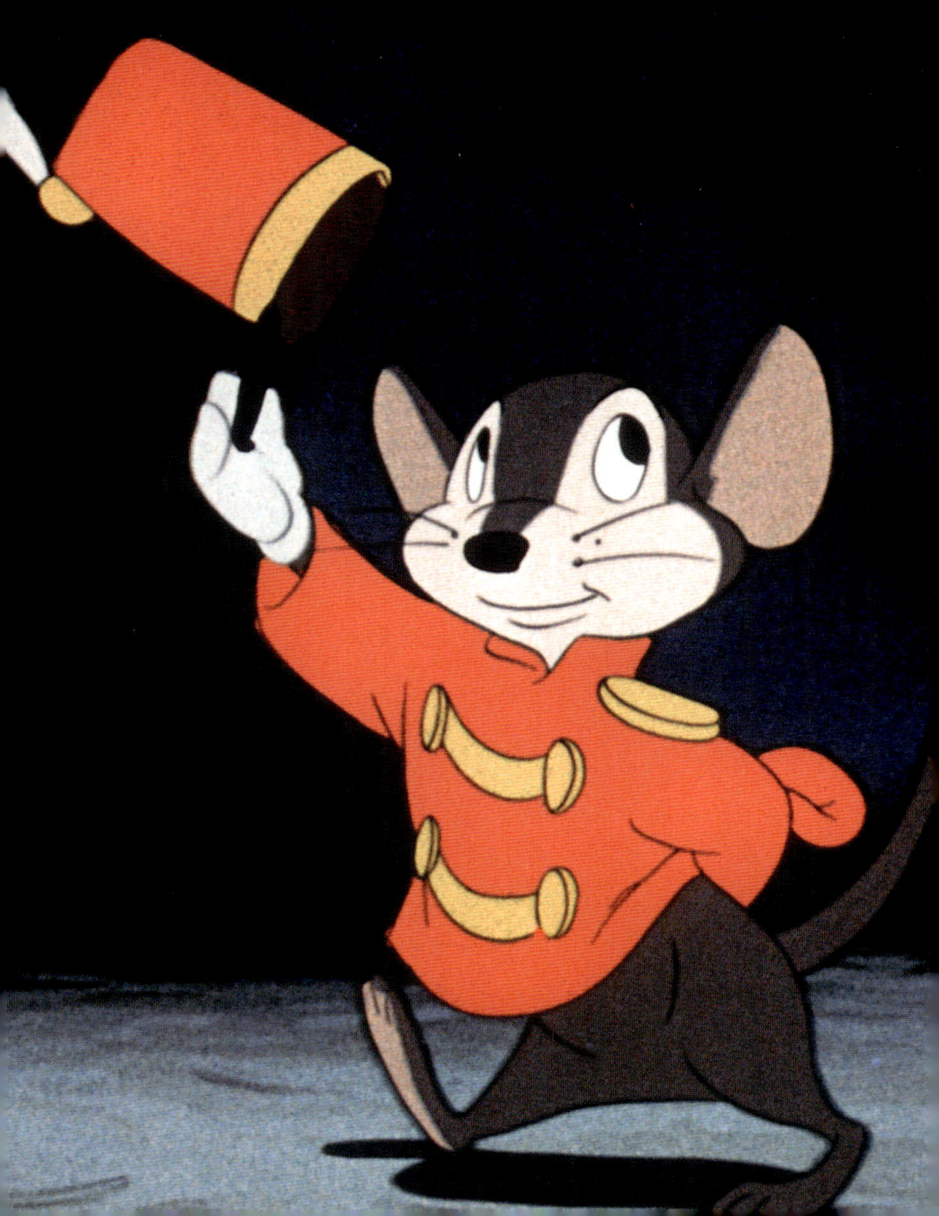

I am imperfectly perfect.

★

Being ashamed of our imperfections can keep us in chains. Break these chains and learn to embrace your flaws. Remember: a big pair of ears may be awkward on the ground, but they can turn into phenomenal wings!

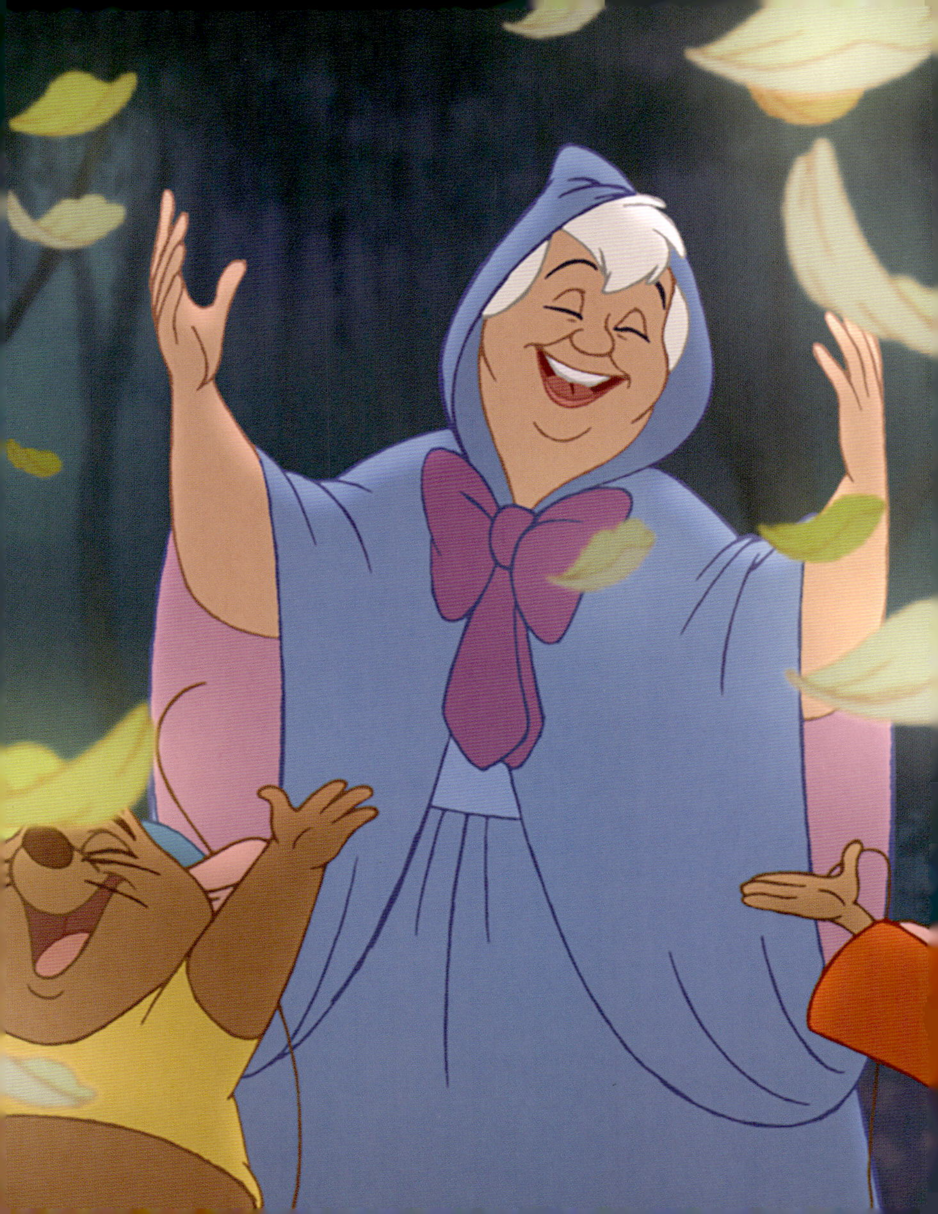

I have magic inside me.

★

It often takes patience and perseverance for the real magic in life to happen. Doing something well requires giving it the time and attention it deserves. Only then will you be able to enjoy its wonderful rewards.

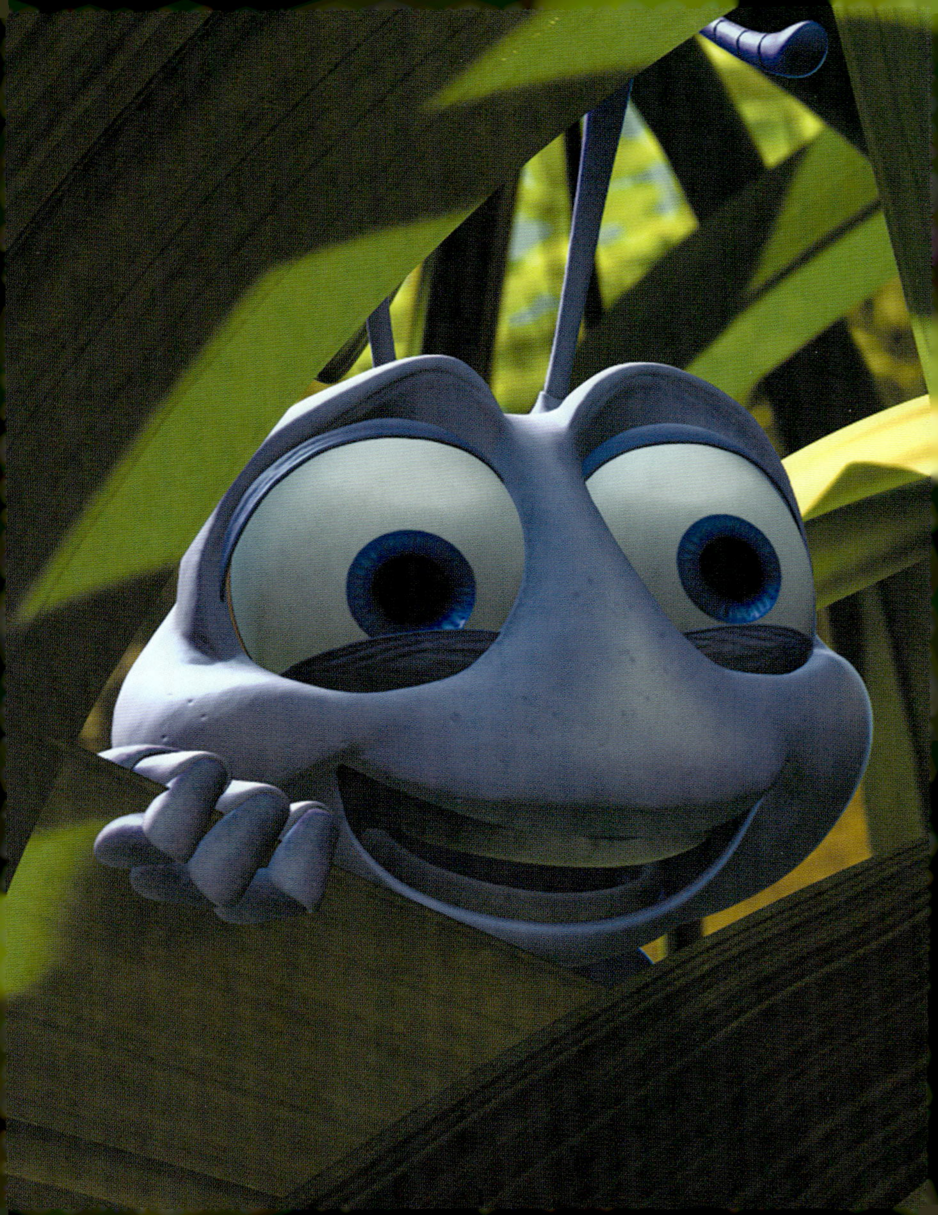

I am powerful.

★

There is hidden promise inside us all, just waiting for the right conditions to sprout. Given sufficient encouragement, this small and secret power within can grow into something no one could have imagined.

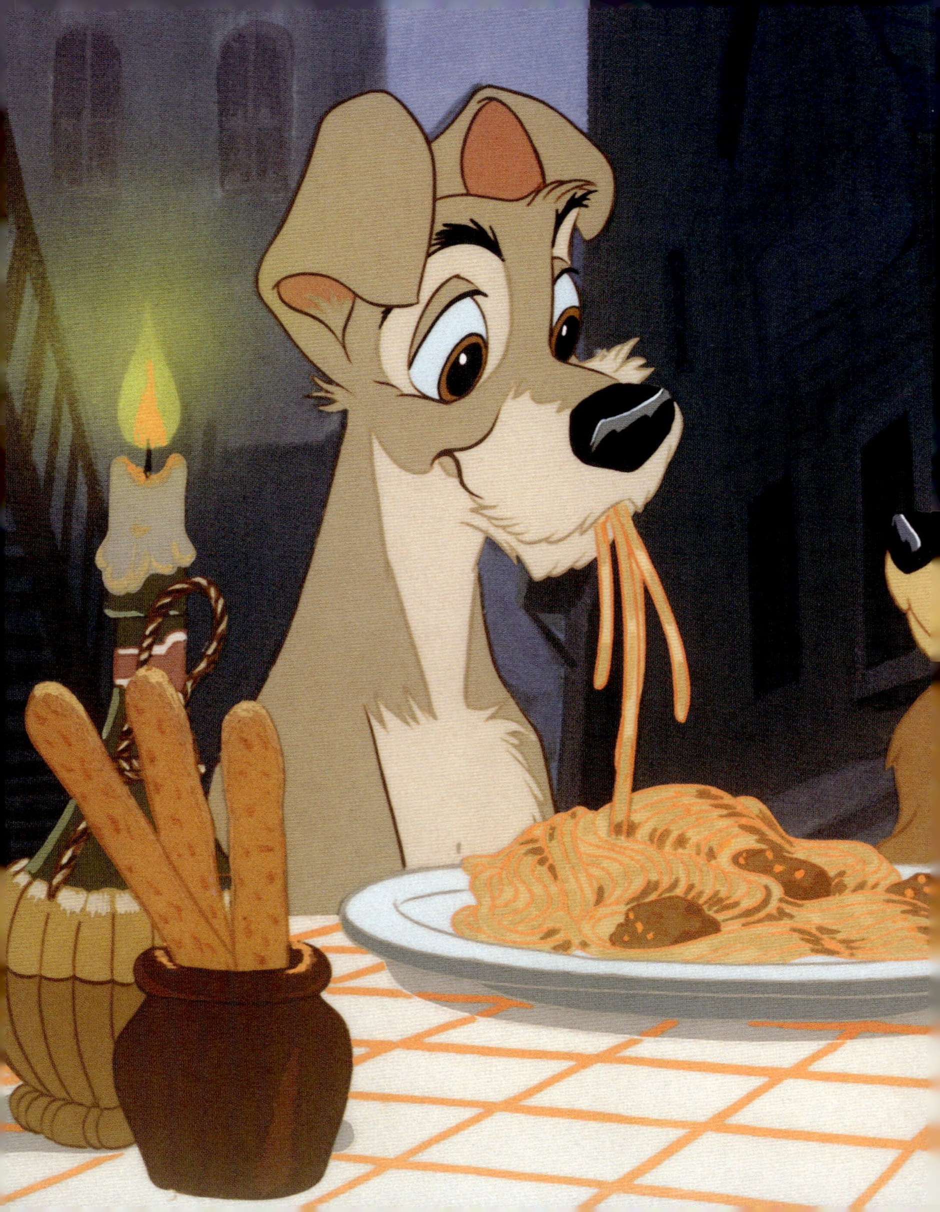

I will make today count.

★

Memories warm the heart and are proof of a life lived fully. So go on, hunt for new experiences. What have you done today that you will remember forever?

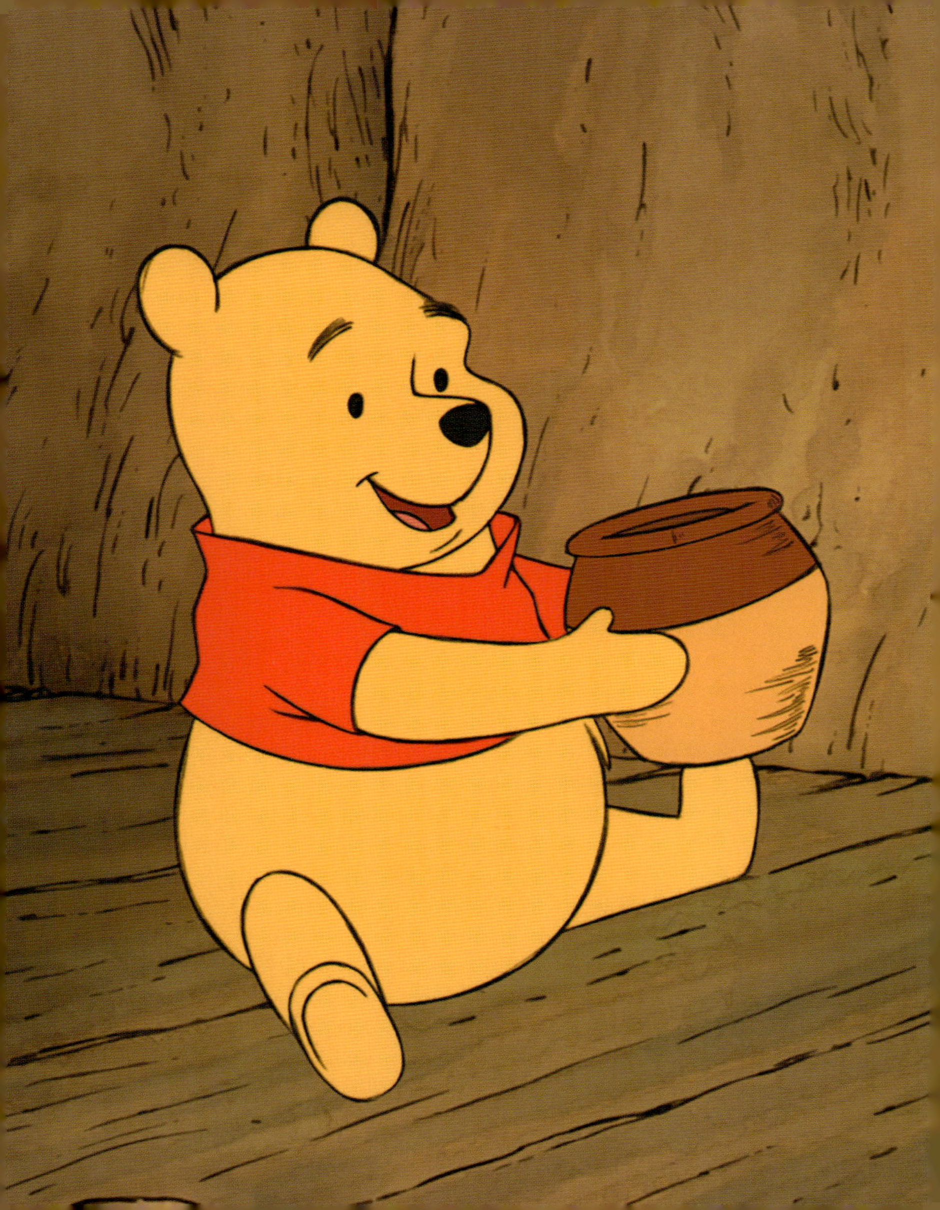

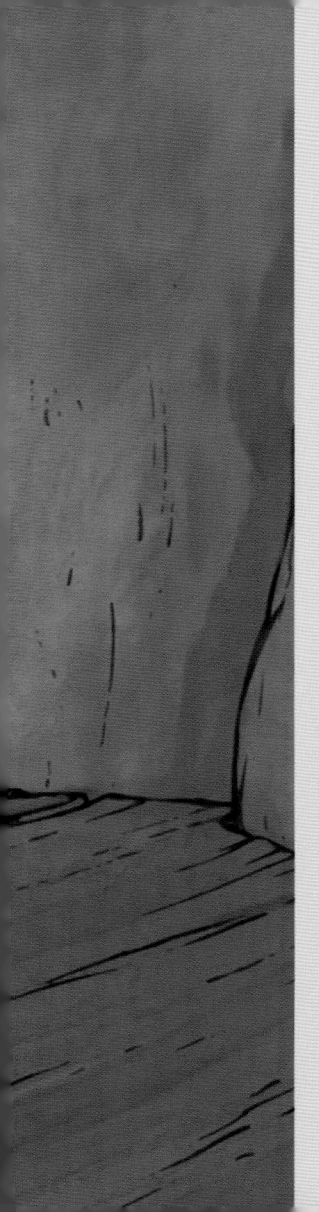

I am excited for my future.

★

The best things happen unexpectedly. Letting life surprise you is the secret to a happy existence.

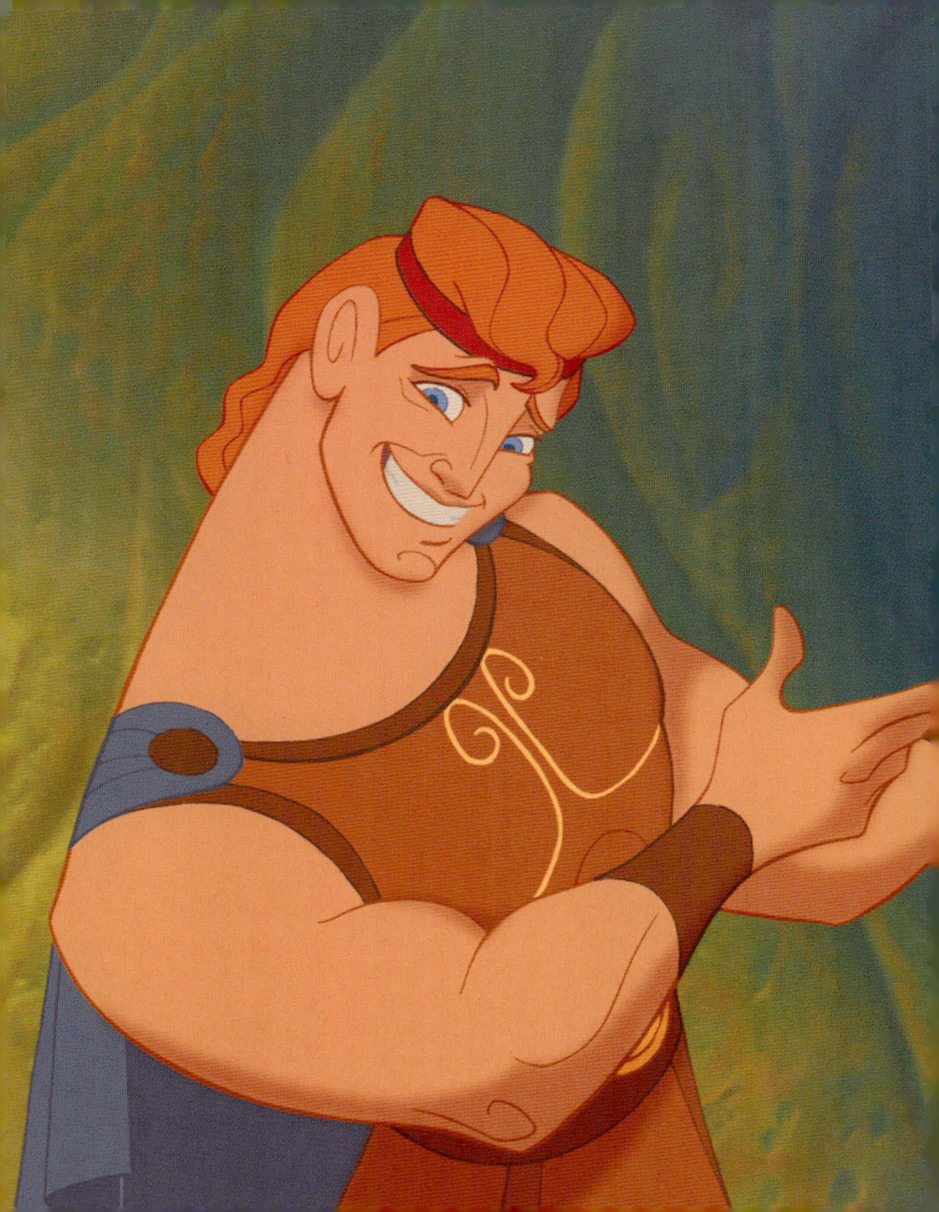

I will find the place I am meant to be.

★

Find your place in the world. It may be in an isolated village or a bustling city, designing aeroplanes or teaching children or managing a business, surrounded by just the right people. Once you find your place, don't let anyone sway you from it.

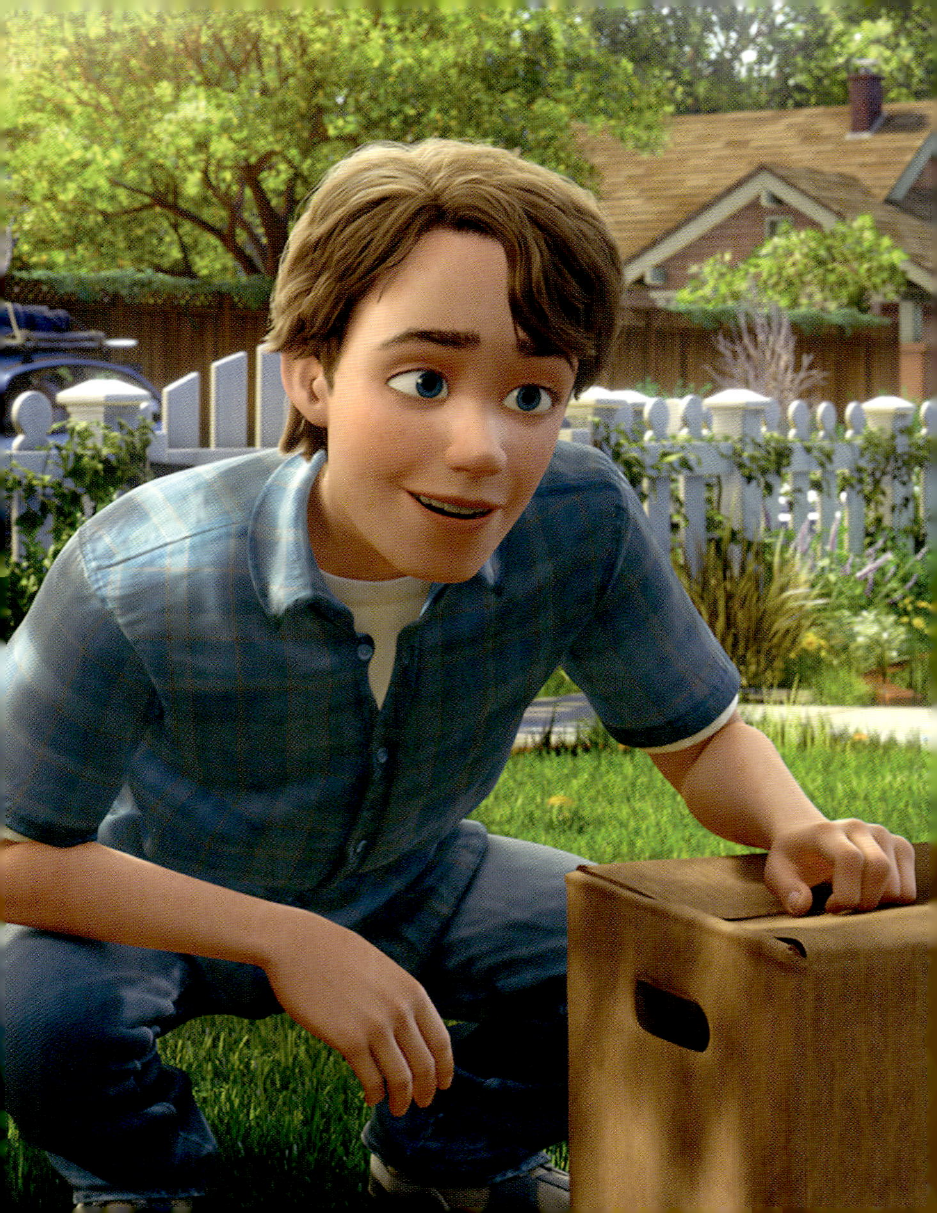

I choose who to trust.

★

Leaving what you have loved in someone else's hands can be tough. Sharing requires trust, care, attention and humanity. Be big-hearted and find a worthy caretaker for your legacy in the world.

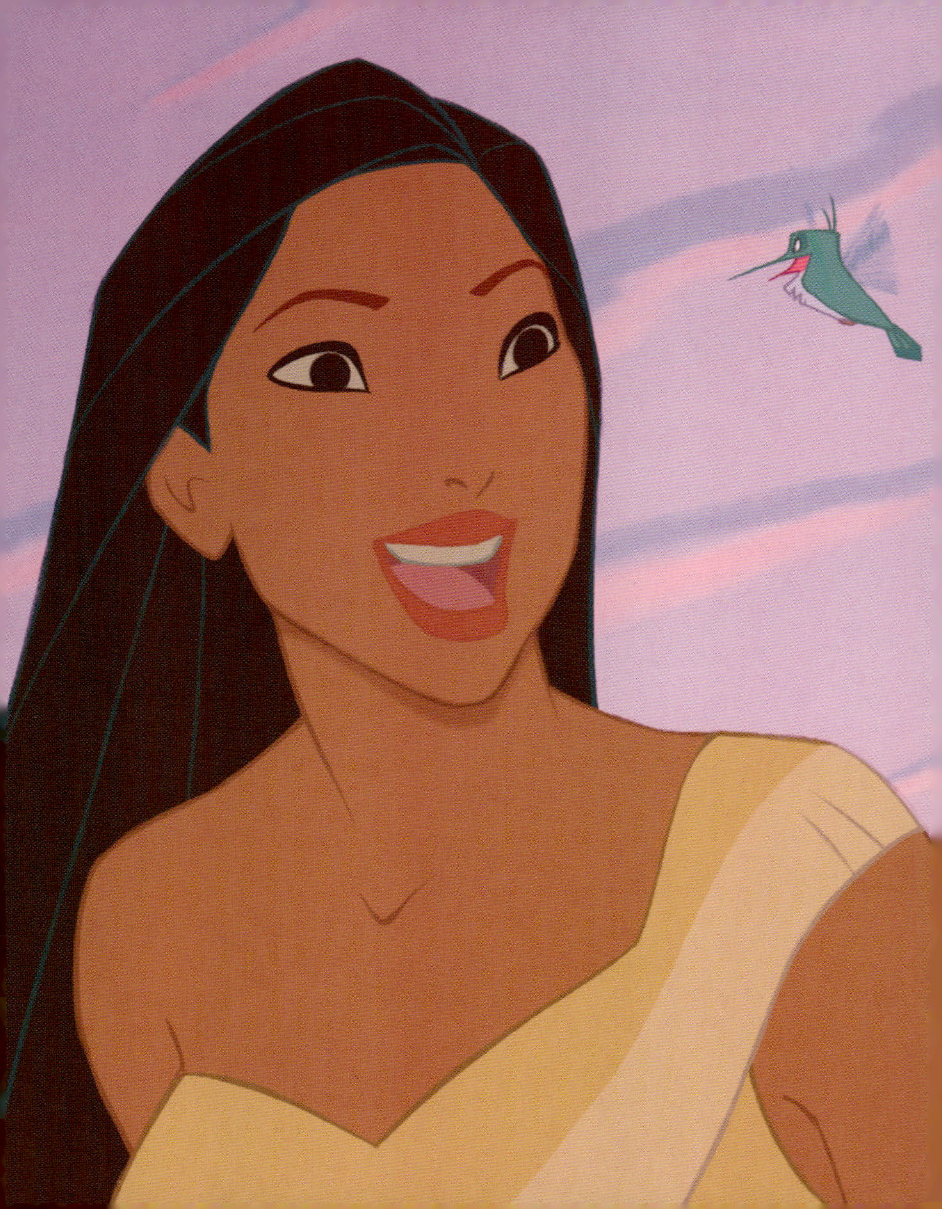

I welcome the wisdom which others have to share.

✦

Let curiosity be your teacher. Discover new sides to yourself by studying and listening to those who are different. Outside of your comfort zone is where the magic happens.

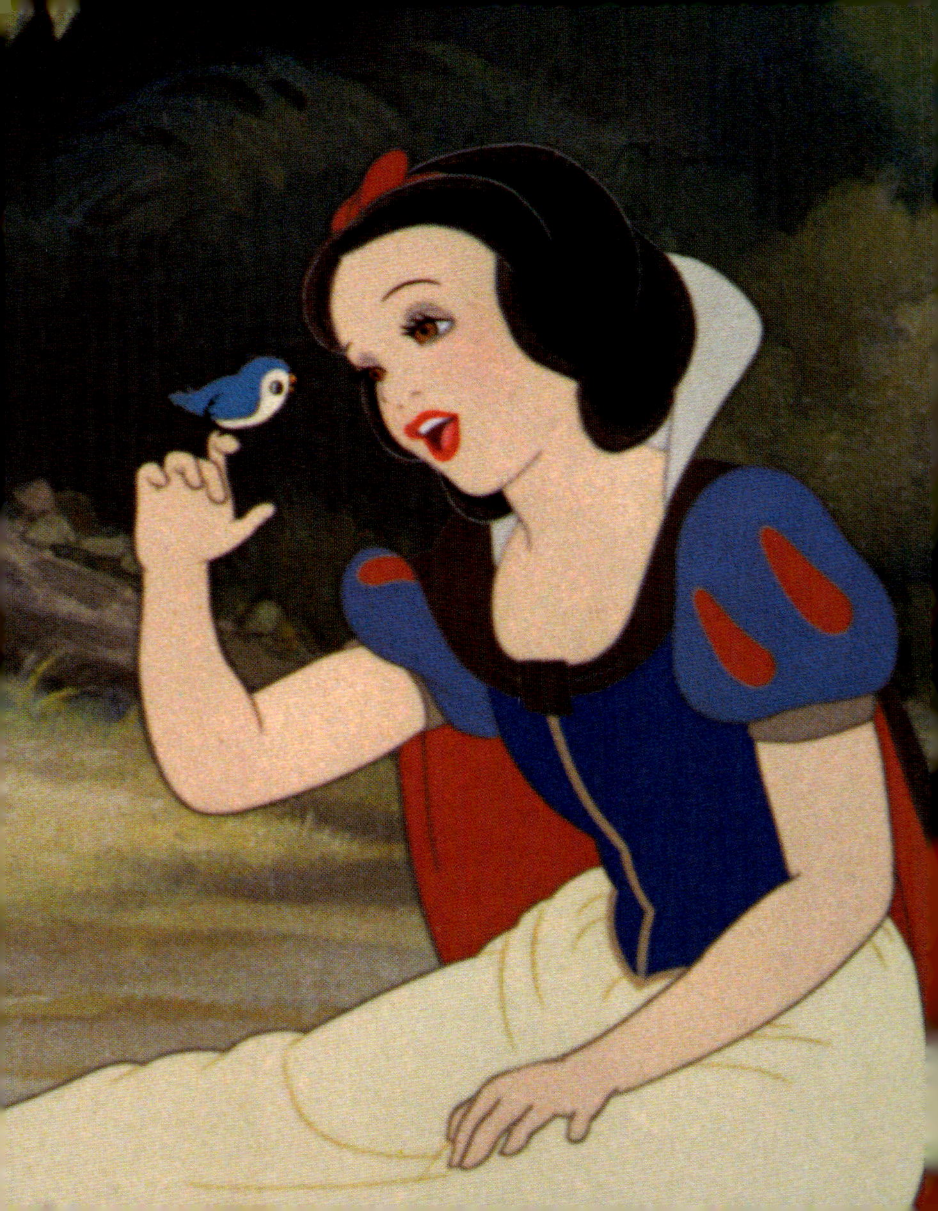

I am cheerful and optimistic.

★

It takes optimism to see that everything's going to be all right. But you can take the first step: a sunny heart and a smile will brighten even the cloudiest of days.

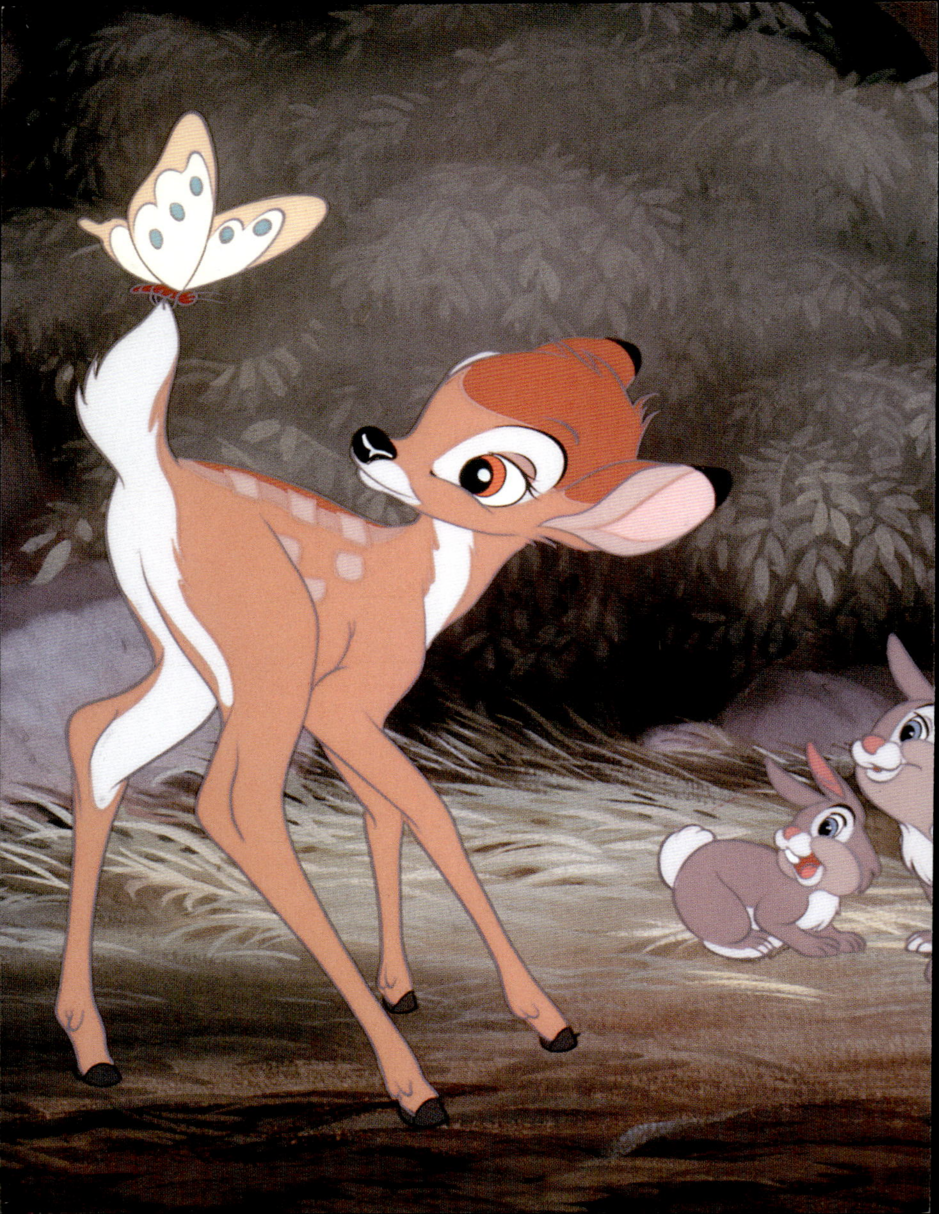

I appreciate the beauty found in the little things.

★

Take notice of the beauty that surrounds you each day. Live your life as a journey of discovery, and the world will forever remain your personal playground.

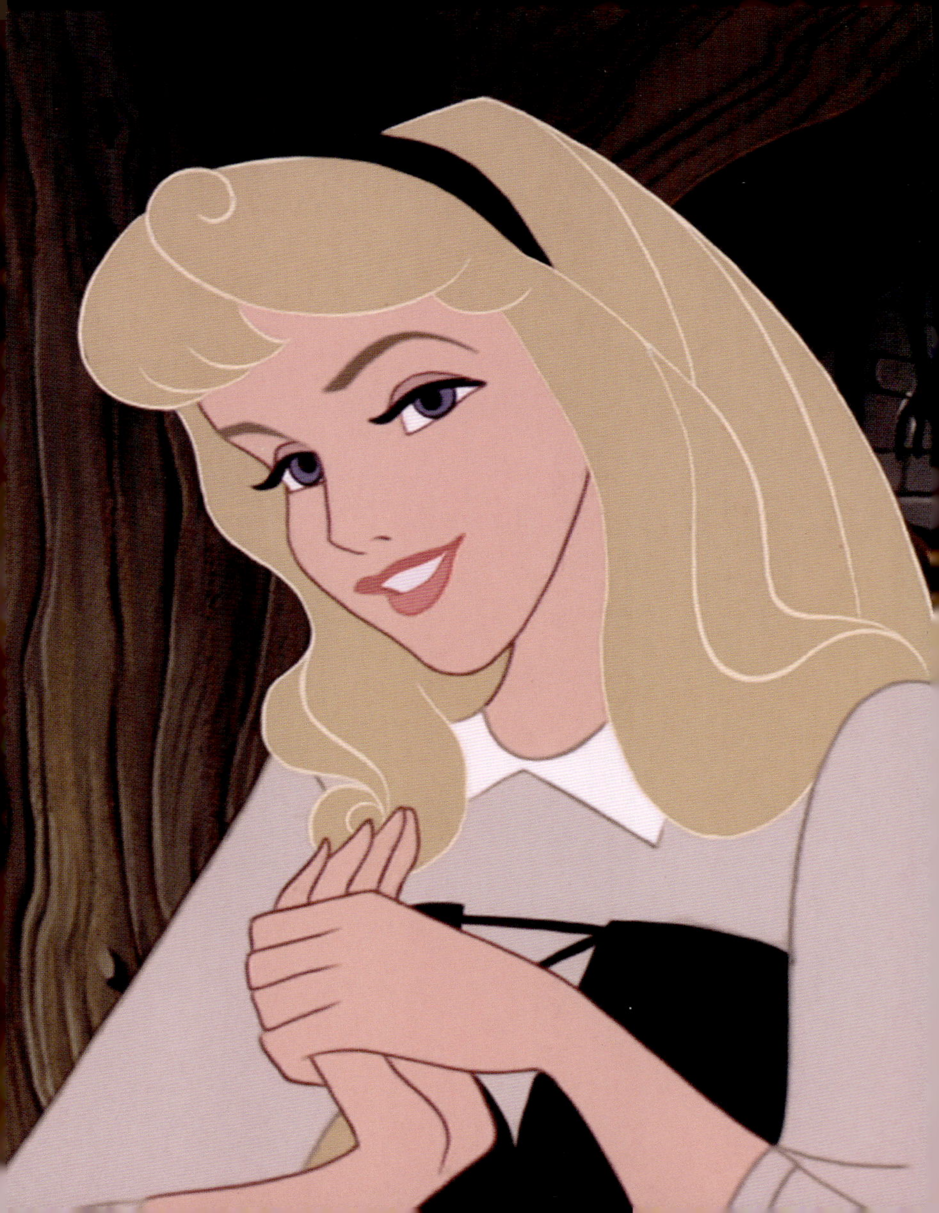

I am focused and determined.

★

Pursuing a dream with passion, commitment and dedication will bring about the magic you need to achieve it. Find the courage to follow your own path, and no one will be able to take it from you.

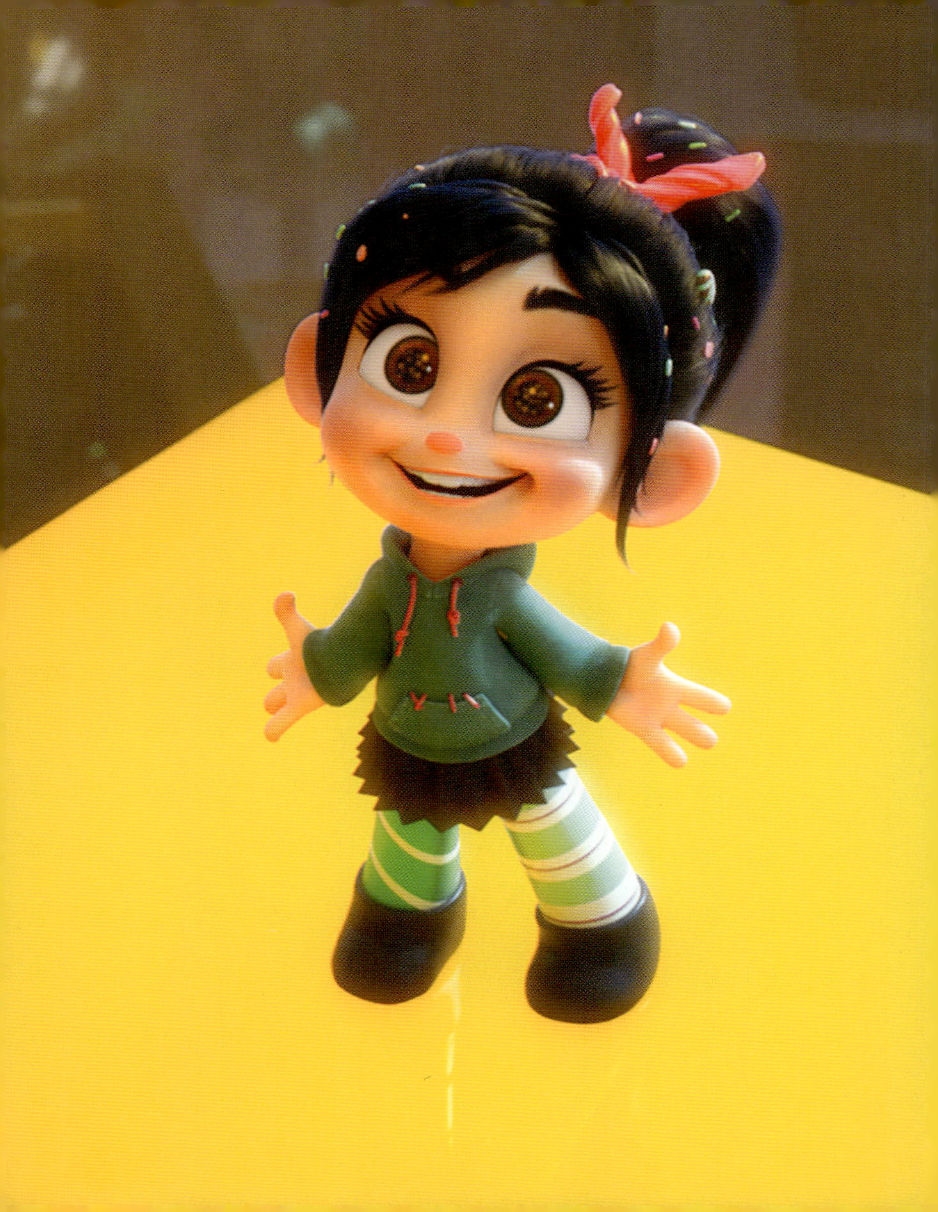

I am ready for any challenge.

★

There is nothing scarier than a boring life. Do not stop dreaming, and always expect more from yourself and those around you.

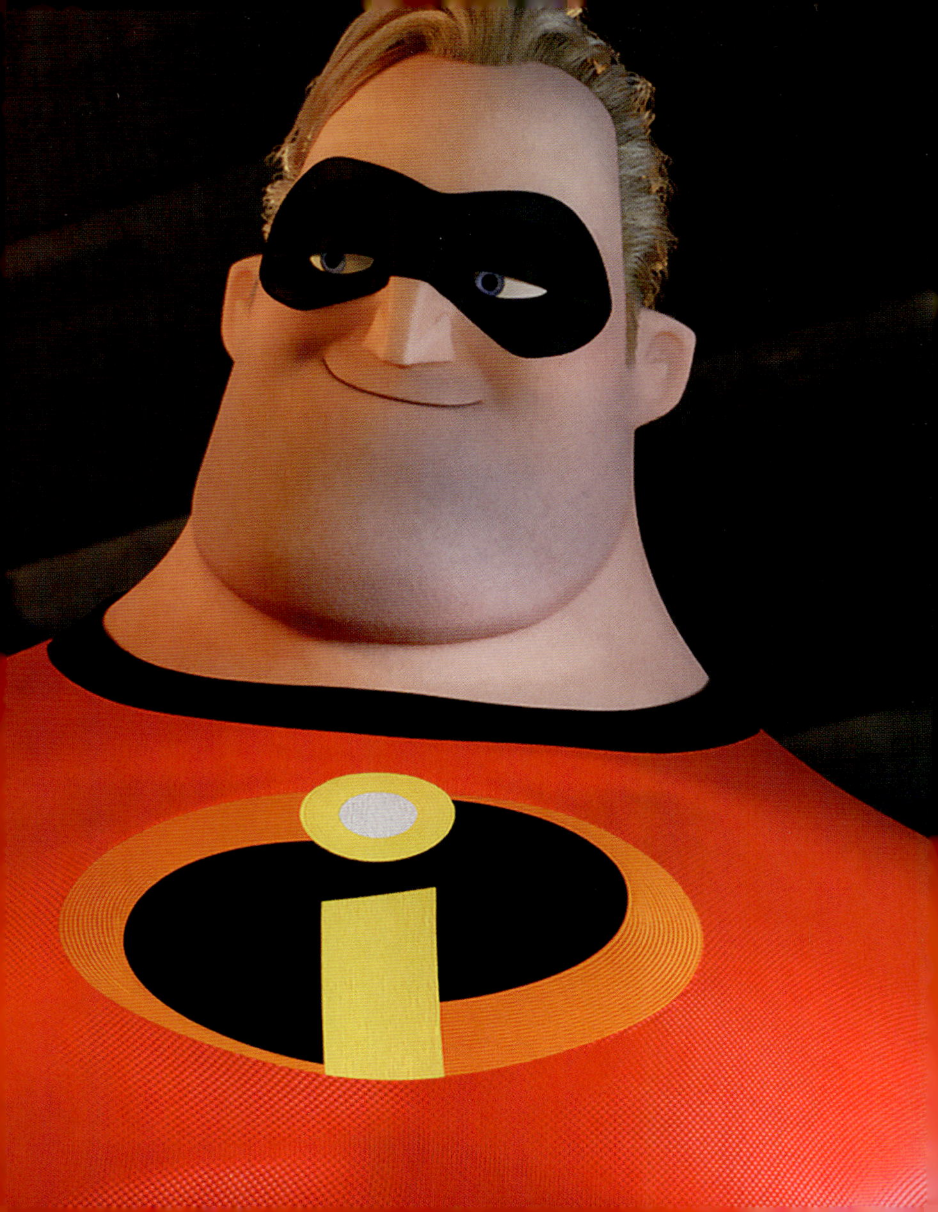

My actions serve not only me but those I am closest to.

★

We all have a great responsibility toward those around us. Turn your "me" into a "we", and you will be able to achieve truly incredible feats!

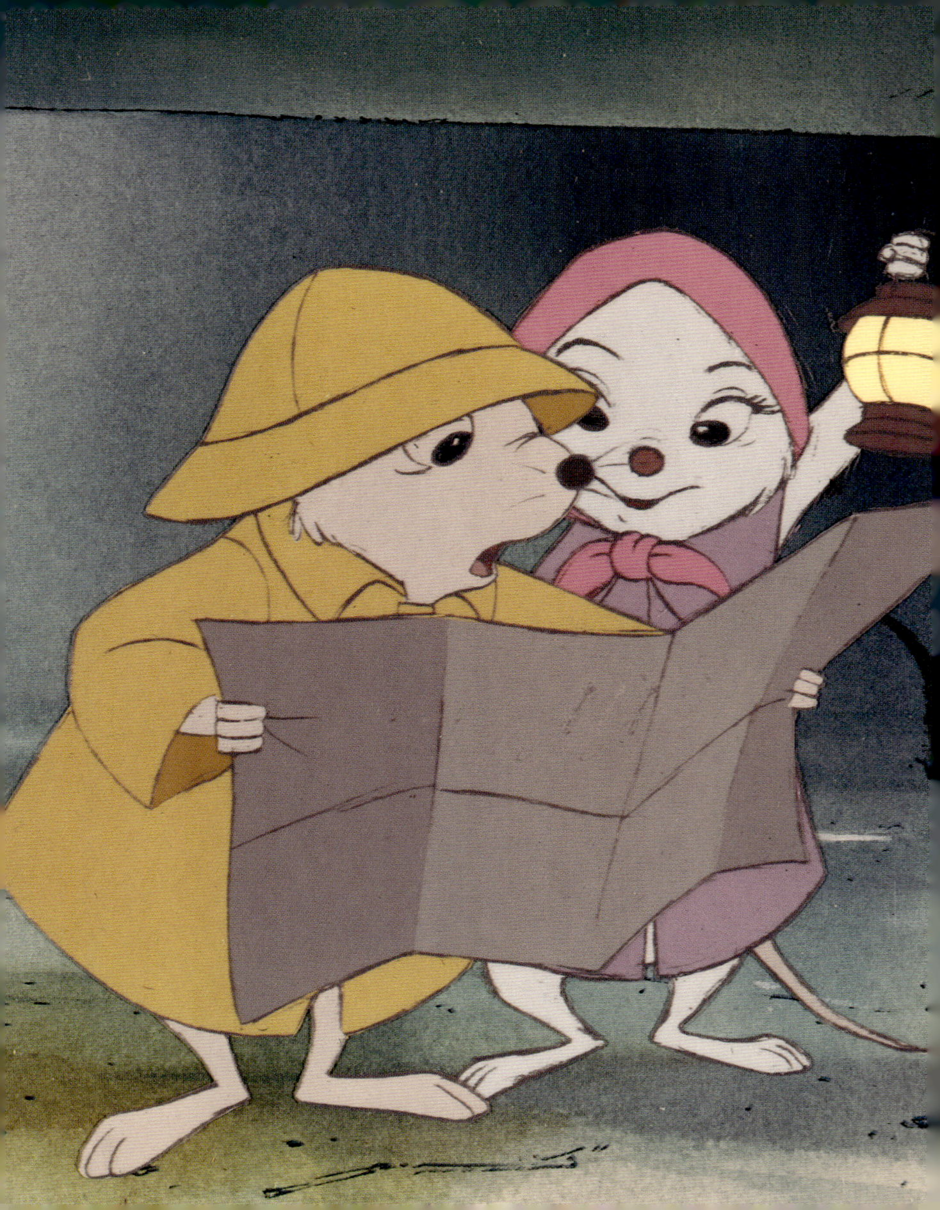

My beliefs matter.

★

Your integrity can falter in challenging situations. Stay true to your values. Your beliefs will be your guiding star when you sail over rough seas.

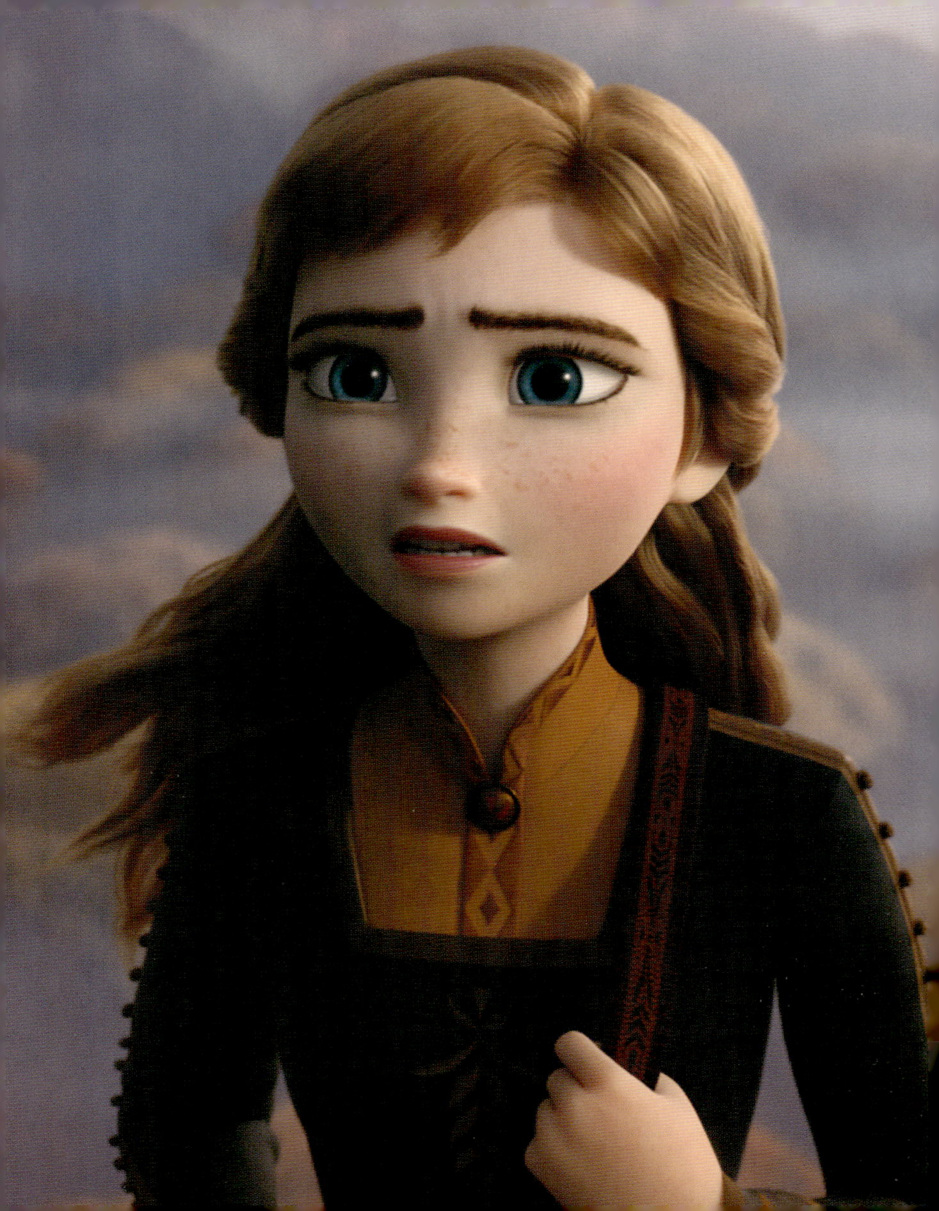

I trust myself to do the right thing.

★

When faced with uncertainty, look at what the next step is. You might not have the right answer, right away, but trust your instinct and it will guide you to a solution.

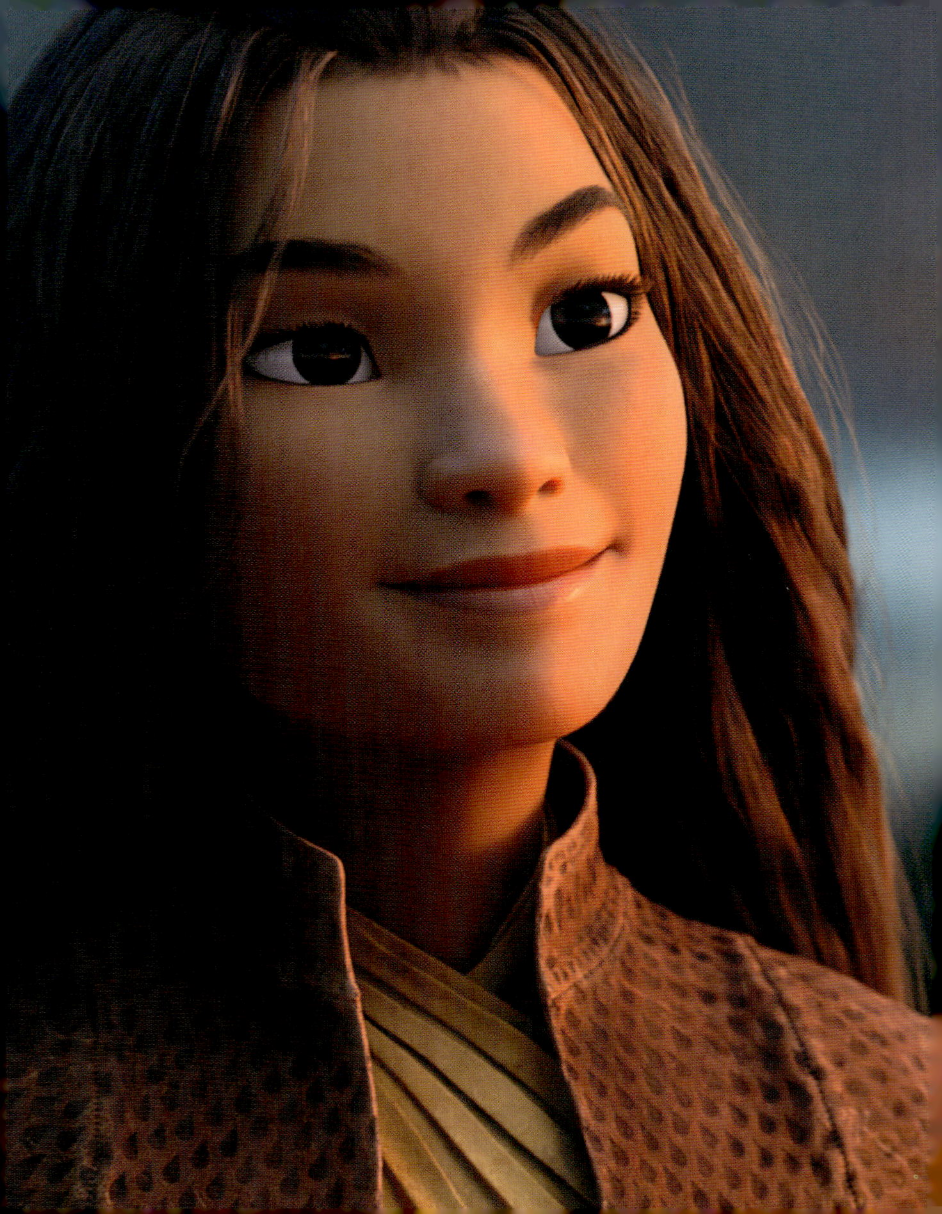

I am equal. Not lesser. Not better.

✸

Embrace the differences offered by other cultures and communities. Living in peace, harmony and unity can lead to a shared success.

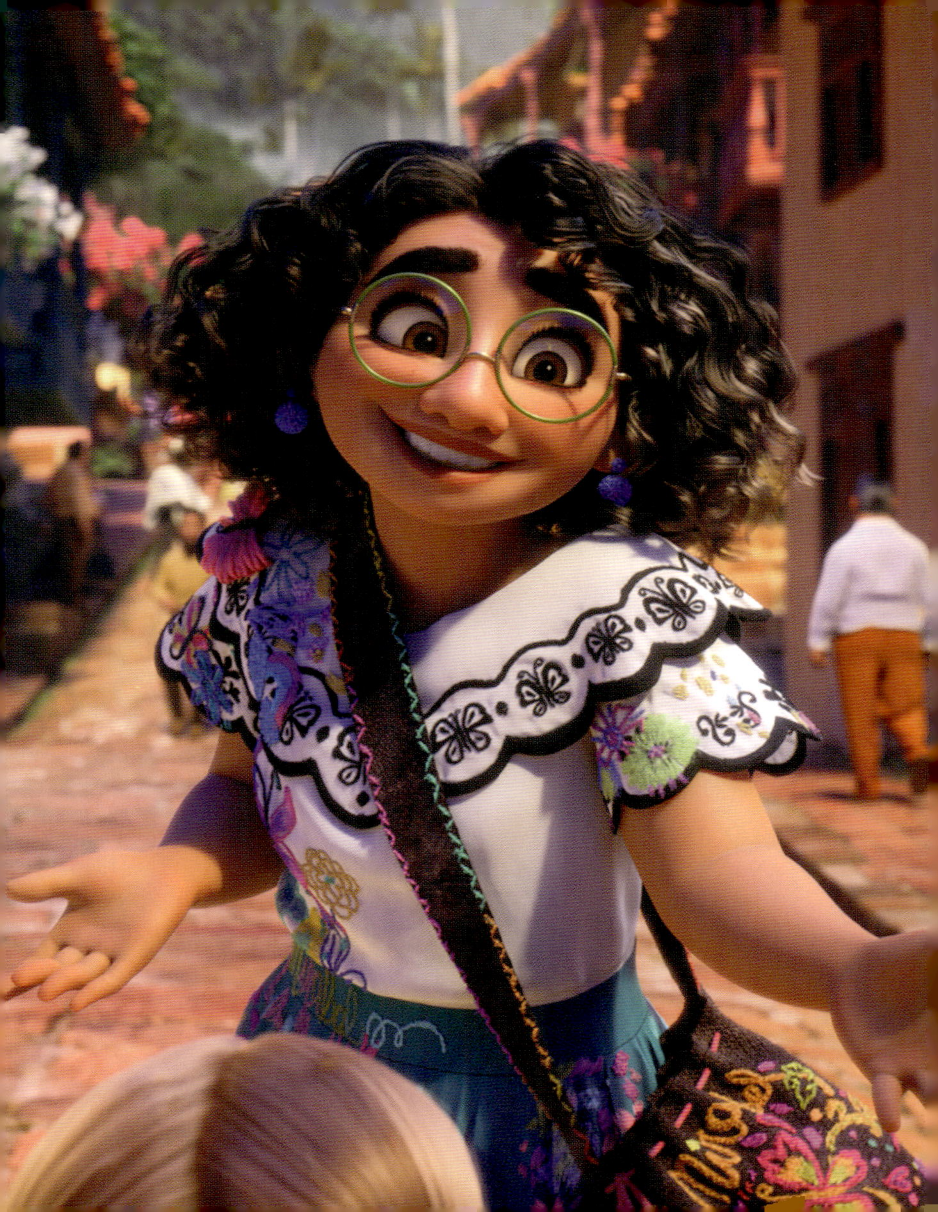

I am a miracle.

★

You are important to yourself and to those who you are closest to. Shine and help others shine too. Your existence is miraculous.

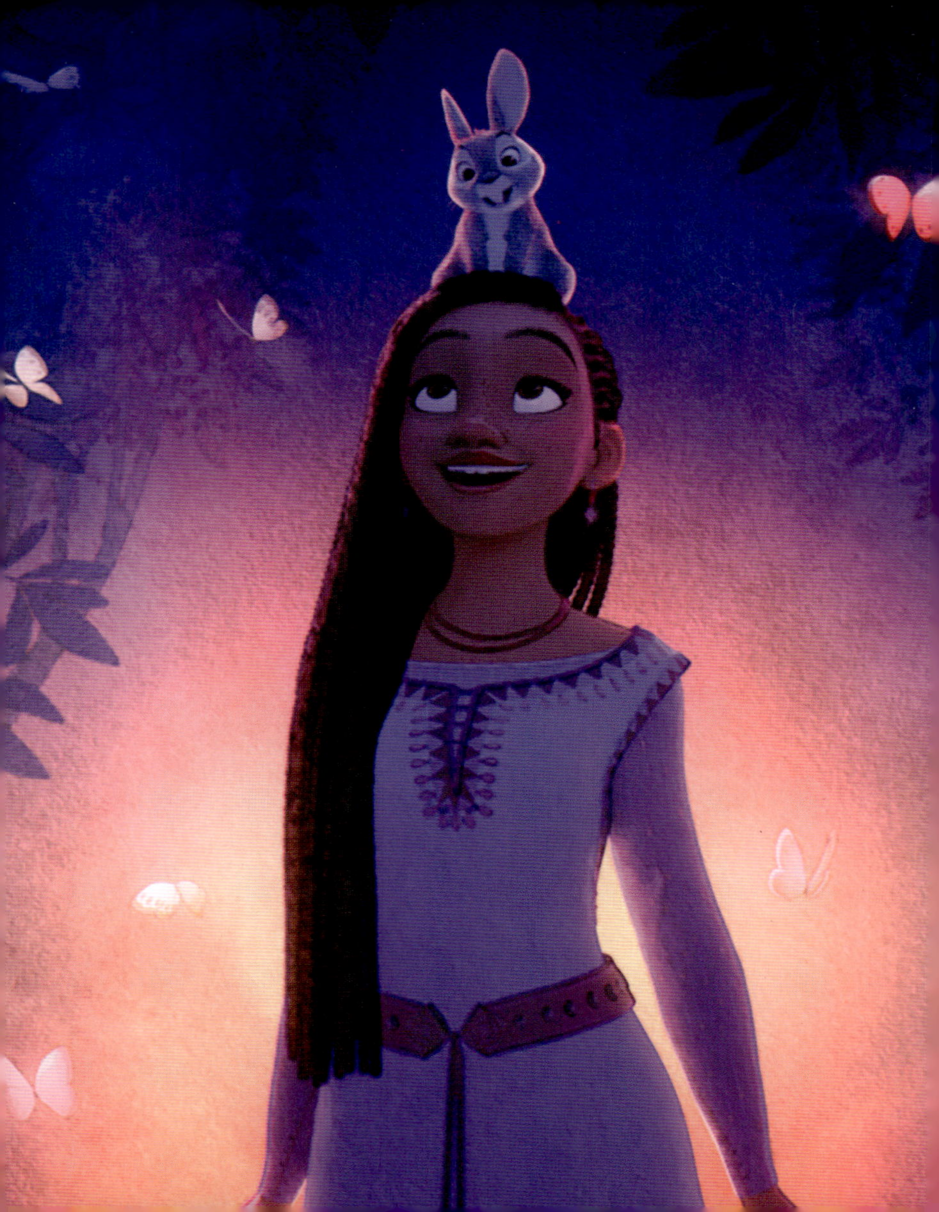

I am made of stardust.

★

The elements in your body were formed inside the stars billions of years ago. You belong in this universe and you are filled with magical stardust.